Nothing ventured, nothing gained

Katie Micuta

All rights reserved, no part of this publication may be reproduced by any means, electronic, mechanical, or photocopying, documentary, film, or otherwise without prior permission of the publisher.

>Published by:
>Best Global Publishing
>PO Box 9366
>Brentwood
>Essex
>CM13 1ZT
>United Kingdom

www.bestglobalpublishing.com

Copyright © 2007 Katie Micuta

Nothing ventured, nothing gained

Nothing ventured, nothing gained

Take some chances; you never know what might happen…….

Always forgive your enemies; nothing annoys them so much.

Oscar Wilde

Katie Micuta

Nothing ventured, nothing gained

For a man with many names,
one of which is King.
For you.

Katie Micuta

Nothing ventured, nothing gained

Chapter one

"Wake up all those sleepy heads out there....it's seven thirty, time to get up," chattered the radio directly into Rosalie's ear, forcing her to open her eyes drowsily and see blurred shapes dance in front of her. She groaned, gave up, and then dropped her head back underneath the comfy darkness of her duvet.
"The news today at seven thirty-three, an accident on the M4 last night caused..."
　　　The talk continued, constantly reminding Rosalie that she should wake up, get dressed and go to work, but she couldn't seem to bring herself to. Too much drink, smoking, loud music and talking last night had made her body feel sore and vulnerable. Her throat ached, her ears rang, her head pounded, and to top it all off, she wasn't sure she had the full use of her legs, as they wouldn't move.
'Maybe I'm in a sleeping bag', she thought sleepily to herself.
"Lee!" a loud male voice shouted up the stairs. She groaned and sunk even further underneath her duvet.
"LEE! Get your ARSE down here!", the voice shouted even louder, more angrily and more impatiently than before.
The sound of footsteps walking up the creaky wooden stairs caused another sound to come from the depth of Rosalie's throat, then the banging on the door made her cry aloud with self-pity.

"Right, I'm coming in, whether or not there's a man in there next to you, or you're not decent." The door opened violently with a gush of wind, lifting various notes on English literature stuck to the walls, photographs of her and her family, posters of her favourite musicians.

"Lee, come on, I've got to get to work." Neus heard a mumble from the bed. "What?"

"I said, I can't get up."

"Course you can, you daft cow," Neus said with an impatient sigh. He hated having to get his sister out of bed in the mornings; she was definitely not a morning person.

"My legs won't move."

Neus rolled his eyes and lifted the duvet with a fierce arm movement. He stood looking down at Rosalie in the foetal position, squeezing her legs up to her chest, her brown hair sticking up from all ends, and her small black vest ridden up to show her green belly piercing.

"That's because you've still got your tights on, and your mini skirt, which I have to say," Neus added while trying to prise Rosalie away from the comfortable dent in the mattress, "is rather too short for your age, young lady."

"Piss off, I'm older than you," she croaked, happily leaving Neus to pick her up and manhandle her to the bathroom.

"You don't act like it, in fact if mum and dad could see you now, they'd be so shocked."

"Yeah, and if they saw the many girls you bring home at night, they'd congratulate you," she said sarcastically, as Neus turned on the shower.

Nothing ventured, nothing gained

He held up his hands in mock innocence. "I've never done such a thing; I'm a virgin, waiting for the right woman."
"Yeah, and I'm a Catholic nun who sits all day praying," Rosalie snorted.
"Well honey, the way you've been going on, that's very hard to believe," he said as he tested the water temperature and twisted some more knobs to make it colder.
"I'm having fun!" she protested. "And anyway, how can you be the one to judge me?"
"I'm not judging, merely commenting." He turned to her. "Shower's ready, see you in a couple of days."
She nodded, then looked up. "Where are you going?"
"Modelling job," Neus said. "In Paris."
"OK. Well, look after yourself," Rosalie said as she turned to the mirror and shrieked at what she saw, her mouth dropping open. She turned back to Neus, standing smugly in the doorway.
"Scary, isn't it?" he said.
Rosalie grabbed the first thing to hand and threw it at him, but the lightweight sponge fell a few inches in front of his feet. He merely raised his eyebrows in a mocking way, showing his amusement at her inability to throw something. Without another word, he turned on his leather loafers and walked away.
"See yah!" he shouted behind him as Rosalie shut the door. She peered back into the mirror reluctantly, scared at what would greet her. If she wasn't already pale and blotchy, Rosalie was sure the colour would have drained from her face, and

if her throat wasn't sore, she would have screamed at this ghost figure staring back at her.

"You can't drink," she said to herself as she grabbed her toothbrush. Various images came back to her mind as she washed her face and untangled her hair. They were blurry but gave the impression that last night was fun, so much fun I can't remember it, she thought reflectively. She and Lesley, her stable friend, jumping on the sofa screaming tunelessly along to "Parklife" by Blur. Playing on Neus's eye toy until the early hours, then the manager of Pitter Patter, Janet, joining and bringing that extra bottle of vodka. Rosalie looked into the mirror once again and sighed. She didn't do well with drink, let alone vodka shots, and she'd been abusing this fact even more recently. She stripped and got into the shower, and gave a yelp of surprise as the freezing cold water fell down her bare back.

"Bastard!" she shouted towards the door. She was sure she heard faint male laughter before the front door slammed.

"Slam the door!" she yelled irritably. It wasn't going to be a good day, she decided.

Neus got into his Jaguar, with a smile still on his face. He loved Lee with all his heart, but she sure could be a moody bitch sometimes. But then, he reflected, that was just amusing. Rosalie had been Lee to him since they were children: in a petty fight he'd said she was a boy and called her Lee to annoy her. The name seemed to have stuck.

Nothing ventured, nothing gained

He started the engine and looked at the road leading him away from his and Lee's modest cottage before pulling out and driving away. He glanced back and smiled: he loved that cottage. Ivy climbed up one side, covering all the red brick, making it look like it was emerging from the sea with seaweed stuck to it. The other side had numerous flower beds and bushes neatly trimmed. He wished he (or Lee) could take the credit for the flowers and the garden, but that had to go to Mrs Baxter, or Gwen, as she told them to call her. Neus knew that he and Lee, or their garden, couldn't have survived this last year without her. Always lending a shoulder or an ear, or even a hand just to hold whenever they needed her to. He was sure that Lee thought of Gwen as their surrogate mother, as their real one was with their father, travelling the world or wherever their father's job took her. Neus's smile abruptly fell from his face as he thought of his parents. At the tender age of eighteen, just a man, his parents had moved him and a twenty-year-old Lee from their current home (which at that time was in France) and brought them to England: more accurately, the small town of Henley-on-Thames.
Neus snorted at the lines they had used: "It's for your own good." "We want you to have stability." Neus wanted to shout at them: "Then quit your job!" But Lee had calmly sat with him when their parents broke the news and listened carefully, asking the appropriate questions in return. Then she had turned to look at his spotty eighteen-year-old face and smiled. Neus knew he would never

forget the kindness and reassurance that had shone in his sister's eyes that moment, and he knew she would look after him. Neus stopped at a traffic light, outside Henley's equivalent to McDonald's, the Wimpy. He looked at the bakery and smelt the fresh bread wafting through his windows and instantly felt hungry. He'd stop and eat when he got onto the motorway, he needed petrol soon. Now at the age of twenty-six, Neus was a successful male model, possessing great looks which other men would die for. With his sandy-coloured hair, apple-green eyes, strong arms and even stronger legs, a flat washboard stomach, his father's olive Spanish skin and his mother's button nose, it was safe to say that women found Neus incredibly attractive. And when a woman got to know Neus, it wasn't just his looks that allured her to him, it was his personality: witty, easy-going, yet serious when it was called for. Neus liked women – that was a fact. He never intentionally caused them pain, but as much as he tried to let them down easily, he'd encountered a few bunny boilers in his time. Thankfully, Lee was always there to calm the women down, make them a cup of tea and discuss things. It always seemed that when the women left, they thought they had dumped Neus.

"How do you do it?" he asked Lee once.

"A woman's mind is a strange thing, little bro, just remember that," she'd replied.

The smile crept back onto his face as he reflected on his relationship with his sister. It was much closer than other ones he had known, and they

Nothing ventured, nothing gained

could share almost everything, confident in the fact that they would both help each other if needed. Neus sped along the motorway, now on his way to Gatwick airport, time to take more pictures and earn his living.

Rosalie stared at the postcard, she was sitting at the bottom of the stairs, nursing a cup of coffee to try to wake herself up before she went to the Acorn stables. She flipped the postcard over in her hands, analysing the beautiful colours of the ocean, all types of blue. Magical, she thought. She looked at the villas on top of the high cliff, overlooking the magical ocean, and saw the circled one. *I am here*, it said by the villa. It was by far the biggest one, with many windows. The massive pool lay in front of the entrance of double patio doors, and wild flowers grew all around the private drive, where the rented Mustang sat. Why have pools when the sea is right there?, she asked herself as once again her eyes were drawn back to the massive blend of blues and many boats sailing past. She flipped the card over and looked at the short, polite, impersonal note. How could he simply send her a postcard and think everything was fine? The cheek! He was playing with her mind, she realised, like he'd done for the last two years. Rosalie snorted as she thought of all the "fun" times she'd had with him. Yeah, hiding in the shadows, secret phone calls, coded text messages, and the sordid meetings, frequently in the park, behind the bushes or even in the car. Never once in either of their houses. Because of

course, that would make it a reality. The "fun" they'd had was special. She put down the postcard and went to the kitchen, washed her cup and dried it using a tea towel. The clock told her she had five minutes before she had to leave and start her day mucking out the horses' stables, gathering the tack for the riders, cleaning it afterwards, washing the bowls, filling up the water buckets – and all for a measly free ride on a Sunday. Any sane person would jack the job in and Rosalie had thought about that on many occasions. But she loved every single second of the hard work. She smiled as she thought of a big clumsy horse which had a special place in her heart and soul. Merlin, with his three white socks and one black one. Merlin, with his liver chestnut coat and shining muscled body. With his kind, emotional eyes that showed his anger and delight. He was a pleasure to ride each Sunday for hacks around the countryside, and for their special rides where they galloped across the fields and up the hills that went on and on. Despite the fact that they were technically trespassing on the Maybrew mansion's grounds and had been told many times to "back off", they still enjoyed the rides and continued to trespass with a smile on both their faces.
Of course, Merlin could do a lot more than hack around the countryside. He was a grade A show jumper, and worked within an inch of his life to please his owner, Mary Blindle.

Mary Blindle….Rosalie hated her, and

Nothing ventured, nothing gained

Rosalie didn't hate many people in her life, with the exception of the writer of the postcard. Mary was one of those women who had it all, yet complained that they didn't have enough. Merlin was just one example of the things she took for granted and didn't really care about. It was such a shame, Rosalie thought, that a horse with Merlin's talent and kind personality was wasted on such a cold-hearted bitch, who had all the gear for horse riding but not a clue how to ride. For Mary, of course, riding was a hobby. For Rosalie, it was her dream to own her own horse, ride it in competitions, dressage and show jumping, even cross-country if she dared herself to. Sadly, she had never had the chance to compete Merlin, in dressage or show jumping, and Rosalie knew she could get the best out of him, better than Mary did anyway. Rosalie put on her lightweight jacket, grabbed her keys and purse, and then made her way to the door, before stopping and staring back at the postcard. She took a tentative step towards it as if it would jump up and bite her. She read the message again and cringed at the signed name, reminding herself that now two people shared the same surname. Rosalie threw the postcard across the room violently, as if to throw him and all the "fun" they'd had with it. She swung out of the door of the cottage and went to Ed. Ed was her car, which she and Neus had named when she'd bought it for £100 at a garage sale. There was no meaning behind the name Ed; they'd both just decided that in the car world it looked like an Ed. Rosalie turned the keys in the ignition and listened in hope for the engine to turn over. After several attempts, Ed eventually spluttered and coughed and came to life. She breathed a sigh of relief. But she knew that eventually, some day, Ed would fail her, like so many others in her life.

Matthew Mason looked up when the knock came at the door. Tili, his assistant, entered timidly, never knowing what type of mood her boss would be in. Sometimes he was pleasant and talkative, sometimes snappish and moody. And at the age of twenty-one, Tili was still getting in touch with her confidence and work experience. This was the first job, apart from the hair salon at the age of fifteen, she'd had that paid the rent and for her much needed Primark suits, bought to please Mr Mason's clients.

"It's all about image in the PR business," Mr Mason had once told her. That evening she'd gone out and found the best Primark suit she could afford. Her eyes met with Mr Mason's and she quickly looked away, trying to suppress a blush she could feel crawling onto her cheeks. It was no surprise to her mother that she had a crush on Mr Mason, as her mother, Joan, had known her daughter would. Mr Mason was a very handsome man, and when Tili went for her first day on the job, Joan had sat her down and explained that Mr Mason was not to be her first boyfriend.

"He uses women," Joan had said.

"Mother, I can look after myself," Tili had assured her, but Joan had just looked at her, knowing her

Nothing ventured, nothing gained

daughter better than she knew herself. Tili hadn't had an official interview with Mr Mason before she was offered the job, because Joan had spoken to Beth Mason, her good friend, and put in a good word for her daughter. Tili had got the job easily. She walked up to Mr Mason's desk and put down the three files.

"Sit," he ordered gently. Tili immediately sat down, crossing her legs and placing her hands in her lap. This is it, she thought, he's going to fire me. Matthew looked at his assistant and noted her discomfort. He wondered if he made her uncomfortable or whether it was his office. He knew that the massive room with oak floorboards and desk, and the solid oak door sometimes intimidated people. Especially the echoing sound that came every time someone spoke, walked, whispered or even dropped a pencil.

"You're doing a great job," he said.

"Oh."

"And I want you to know that."

"Ok."

"And I would like you to feel at ease with the job and the clients, so if there's a problem, please come to me." Matthew gave her the famous Mason grin that usually had women falling at his feet or their mouths hanging open. Tili was no exception.

"Oh, um, thank you....I will...." she said, flustered that he kept grinning at her. She got up to leave, even though she couldn't trust her legs, and then remembered something.

"Oh, Mr Mason..."

"Matthew," he interrupted.
"Oh, um, Matthew then, a Mr Foster called, he said it was urgent and you needed to call him back."
"Kevin?" Matthew asked, clearly happy that his best friend had called.
"Yes. He said it was urgent business."
"OK, I'll give him a call. Thank you Tili," he said, then returned to his work. Tili knew when she'd been dismissed.

Beth Mason looked at the portrait of her darling husband. Lord, he had complained about having to stand for that long! His strong, confident face, which held a certain arrogance, frowned back at her in the way only he could. That stare: something so compelling, something that would kill anyone who dared to cross him. It made him seem strong and so powerful, even scary. Only a few people had known the real man like she and their son Matthew did. Ah, Matthew! Now there was another man who had that stare and that handsome face. People had wondered in the past if she was actually his mother, as he had not inherited any of her looks; unless they got to know Matthew, when they would have noticed Beth's kind, helpless romantic nature which he had inherited. It was unfortunate, thought Beth, that no woman had yet experienced Matthew's romantic nature. Apart from one woman, but then, she and Matthew never talked about her. It was her one wish to see a woman catch his eye, though, see the woman who would bewitch her son and make

Nothing ventured, nothing gained

him lose the hard edge he used for business and seemed to use for everyday life. She'd be someone special, who would keep him guessing, someone who would stand up to him, fight him and not back off like so many of Matthew's past girlfriends had done. The girls he had brought home: some so boring, some so weepy, some so clingy it made Beth feel sick. And she could see that Matthew didn't appreciate these qualities either. He was, as they say, passing the time with these girls. But she couldn't blame Matthew for losing faith in romance and love after his past experience, which had hurt him to depths at which Beth could only guess. He hadn't tried to look for anyone else. Since Beth had found out the doctor's results, she's made it her priority to find Matthew a woman. She knew she couldn't very well arrange a marriage, but if she rang a few people, called in a few favours, she was sure some woman out of the bunch she had picked would catch his attention. She looked up at her husband's face again. She had loved him dearly when he was alive, and had continued loving him even though he was no longer there. Their love was special and would go on for ever, of that she was sure. Now, all she had to do was get Matthew to experience the same love she and his father had.

"Kevin!" Matthew exclaimed into the telephone receiver.
"Matt, oh God, am I glad it's you."
"What's up?" Matthew said and leant forward as

he heard the urgency in Kevin's voice.

"I can't tell you on the phone – it's too personal, private, even fucking dangerous."

"OK," Matthew said slowly. "Where do you want to meet and talk about it?"

"Pitter Patter, the restaurant in Henley, tomorrow night, and...Matt, I'm sorry about putting you in this position."

Matthew laughed unsurely. "God, you've not killed anyone, have you?"

There was silence, in which time Matthew's face went pale.

"No, although someone's life could be in danger if I don't sort this out, and you are the only man who can help me."

"I get it, because I'm your best friend?"

"Hell no, because you have connections, money and you're good at keeping secrets," Kevin answered, laughing.

"Is that a sarcastic answer?" Matthew asked.

"Um...I'm not too sure. Maybe you should decide on that one."

"Look, Kev, give me a clue as to what this is about."

"Women, money, houses....secrets." Kevin said the last clue slowly, letting the emphasis and meaning sink in for Matthew. Matthew didn't smile as he added, "Tomorrow, seven. Don't be late," then slammed the phone down.

Nothing ventured, nothing gained

Chapter two

Rosalie got out of Ed and walked up the gravel towards the block of stables. She lifted her head and squinted towards the sky. She smelt freshly cut grass and a faint scent of magnolia fly spray, as she looked towards Merlin's empty stable, leaving her in no doubt that he'd been put out in his field. Rosalie sighed. She loved having the battle with Merlin in the morning about which rug to put on, and she loved the way he nodded his head up and down to show his impatience. In fact, she just loved everything about him.

"Lee!" Rosalie looked around at her name being called and saw Lesley standing there, tacking up Jasper, a big strawberry roan, and walked over to her.

"Yeah?" she croaked. Lesley laughed.

"You sound as bad as I feel. Good night though, wasn't it?" she asked, gathering the saddle off the rack.

"It was. But I regret it now."

"Why?"

"Well...I feel incapable of speech, of walking, and if I think, those tiny wheels in my mind hurt to move."

Lesley laughed again and tutted at Rosalie.

"You can't hold your drink," she said as she gently pushed the bit into Jasper's mouth.

"How did you guess?" Rosalie asked sarcastically, but smiling all the same.

They were both silent for a moment as Lesley did Jasper's girth up and the big horse snorted and scraped the floor.

"Jasper!" shouted Lesley. He immediately stopped scraping the floor, but Rosalie could have sworn she saw the mischief in his eyes.

"We're galloping across the Maybrew again today, want to join us?"

Rosalie thought about it for a minute, looking down at her shoes, then shook her head.

"You have to ride another horse sometime," Lesley pointed out.

"But I only want to ride Merlin."

"It's good to gain experience from other horses."

"I don't want other horses, I want Merlin." Even though Rosalie knew she sounded like a child stamping her feet and demanding more ice cream, she couldn't help it.

"Christ, you are hung over." Lesley mounted Jasper from the ground, gathered up her reins and both of them walked away. Rosalie went to work mucking out Merlin's stable first, before any of the others she was meant to do. She paid extra care to Merlin's; it had always been that way. Flattening the shavings, making the surface look irresistible and tempting to snuggle up in, then filling the buckets of water up to the rim, to make sure he never went thirsty. Rosalie left Merlin's clean stable and started on Betty's. Betty was a small grey Welsh pony, with an ever-expanding hunger and a massive attitude problem. Betty was kind at heart, but when forced to work for her owner she could throw all the rears, bucks and spokes that a horse could. Rosalie put on her iPod and started playing the Beatles. She sang tunelessly along to

Nothing ventured, nothing gained

the words of "Strawberry Fields Forever" and began swaying and dancing with her mucking-out fork.
"Nothing to get hung about…..living is easy with eyes closed!" she bellowed, happy to be feeling better and happy that the sun was shining. Life wasn't that bad, she decided, especially when she had a new job at a restaurant and had the house to herself to chill out tonight. She would watch *Eastenders* all curled up under her massive duvet with a bar of chocolate, and strawberries, and a nice big, takeaway pizza, which would have been delivered, so she could have a bath and get into her Snoopy PJs. Rosalie was so engrossed in her dancing and singing that she hadn't noticed a woman hovering uncertainly by the stable door.
"No one I think is in my tree…" Rosalie continued to sing and twirled around, flinging the fork out with her. She felt it make contact with something and her eyes snapped open. It was then she saw a young woman rubbing her leg and looking as if she might cry.
"Shit!" Rosalie exclaimed, and pulled the earphones out roughly, as she went to the woman's aid.
"I'm so sorry, I was in a world of my own," she explained, trying an embarrassed laugh.
"Yes, well, I can see that," the woman snapped, still rubbing her leg.
"Can I help you to a chair?" Rosalie offered.
"No. I just came by on the orders of my boss." When Rosalie didn't answer, the woman continued. "He and his family wish that your horse

riders would not, and I mean NOT", Rosalie winced at the repeated word, "ride on the Maybrew grounds again. It turns up the grass and makes it look dreadful for the summer, when, as you are aware, there is hardly any rain and the grass doesn't grow back."

"Hold on…I don't ride up there, OK? If your boss wants to make a point, ask him to come down personally. Or write a letter to the manager of this yard." Rosalie wasn't about to admit to riding on the Maybrew grounds, but she was damned if she was going to be told what to do and it annoyed her that her good mood had now worn off.

The sound of "Lucy in the Sky with Diamonds" could be heard now as the silence between the two women continued. Finally, the other woman straightened up and lifted her chin higher.

"What is your name?" she asked politely.

"Rosalie."

"Are you the manager?"

"No."

"Can you tell me who is?"

"No," Rosalie answered, matching the polite and slightly patronising tone of this young woman.

"And can I ask what your name is?"

"Tili."

"Right, well, Tili, I suggest you pass my message on to your boss and until we come to some sort of arrangement, people will continue to ride on the Maybrew grounds. So I guess it's in your best interest to get this sorted, as it's spring now and summer isn't far away."

Tili looked angry, but then the fire in her eyes

Nothing ventured, nothing gained

suddenly went out and she began crying. Rosalie first felt shock, and then a massive rush of guilt swept over her. She looked at Tili and realised she must be in her early twenties, and probably new to this job.
"Shit, I'm sorry," Rosalie began, but Tili just lifted her head and wiped her eyes.
"No, I'm being stupid." Tili's head went down again. "But, oh God, I want to be so good at this job, but I can't deal with people, you know?"
Rosalie didn't get a chance to answer as Tili carried on talking.
"I just...well...I think I stand a good chance with him and if I screw this job up, he's not going to be interested in me, is he?"
Rosalie thought back to how she'd felt when she'd been in a similar situation. Having to prove herself, make him feel like he needed her, and trying to be something she wasn't. "I hate him", she thought, "I hate that postcard, I hate the fact that he still has a hold over me and I HATE him!".
Rosalie suddenly realised that Tili was still talking. "My mummy wants us to be together and I'm sure his does as well. I just....man, if I keep crying like this in front of people I definitely won't be strong enough for him, will I?" She looked at Rosalie.
"Well...um..." Rosalie wasn't sure how to answer.
"Oh, forget it. I'll give Mr Mason your message and I'm sure he'll pay you a visit. I'll give him your name and you can take him to who's in charge."
"OK," was all Rosalie could say.
"Well....bye." Tili walked away fast, her face reddening with embarrassment and shame at how

much she had exposed to a total stranger. She just didn't know what came over her. She couldn't hold those tears in any more.

Rosalie watched the girl walk away and felt sad again. "I Am the Walrus" wafted through the air as she finished the stable and closed the door.

"Lee, there's a phone call for you," shouted a voice from the coffee room.

She walked to the telephone and picked it up with a flat "Yeah?"

"Man, you sound happy!"

"Donny!" she exclaimed, suddenly happy for real.

"Hey babe, I've missed you, but guess what? I'm back!"

"That's great!"

"Yeah, and I need a place to stay, so I wish I could say this is totally personal, but it's actually a case of an emergency."

"Why?"

"Well….I was talking to this hot girl..."

"Woman," corrected Rosalie.

"Yeah, whatever. Anyways, so I was talking to her, using the old Donny charm, and then her massive rugby-built husband comes up and puts his arm around her."

"Oh God, you're alright, aren't you?"

"Me? I'm in one piece. But you should have seen the carnage I caused when he went for me. People were whistling their support."

"Did you hurt him?" she asked, cringing at the possibility of a big rugby man looking for Donny in the middle of the night and turning up at her house.

Nothing ventured, nothing gained

"No. I just ran like a fucking Olympic sprinter and the carnage was all my clothes over the floor in my desperate escape route."
Rosalie laughed. "Oh Donny, you really are a prat.
"I'm a prat, but I'm a fast-moving prat," he said and she could tell he was smiling.
"So, I'm guessing you need somewhere to stay?"
"Why else would I call?"
"Because you love me?"
"Ha! My love comes with conditions."
"Such as?"
"A bed for the night. I don't mind if it's with you, I'd like to feel your body pushed against..."
"Donny," she warned, with a smile.
"Oh OK, I guess I could cope with the sofa," he said, laughing.
"I'm at the stables at the moment, but I'll be home at about six. Is that OK?"
"Sure, I'll just hang around."
"Well...yeah, you have to, 'cos I'm not coming back to let you in yet."
"Maybe I could break in, my little friend."
"Uh-huh," she answered doubtfully.
"I have my ways," he said mysteriously before he hung up. Rosalie smiled as she replaced the receiver and started on her next stable.

Beth Mason looked out of the window at the horse galloping away from their grounds and, if she weren't mistaken, in a guilty way. She had to do something about those riders, yet she understood why they wanted to ride on her grounds. They were spectacular and perfect for riding, and Beth could even understand that people didn't want to ride on the roads, especially with all the accidents that happened these days. She saw young Tili walk up the drive and glance up at the clouded sky. Beth couldn't help but feel sorry for her. She was so young and had so many dreams and aspirations, one of which was her son. She'd decided already that it wasn't to be Tili, she was too young, vulnerable and also so incredibly wet that it got on Beth's nerves. She'd only agreed to take Tili on because her good friend Joan had pleaded on Tili's behalf.

"She will never get out if she doesn't have this job," Joan had said to her.

"Do you think she would appreciate you pleading for her like this?"

"No, but she should be bloody grateful," Joan had replied.

Beth thought it sad that she would want to get rid of her daughter, but Tili wasn't the most responsive person she had met. She sighed. It was rather annoying that Matthew didn't find a woman and that she had to take action. He had always been like that when he was little, yet when it came to making decisions and using his head, he needed no encouragement from anyone. He had shown himself to be the rock in the family since they had moved here in 1995 and definitely hadn't faltered when it came to keeping the story that he and his father had agreed to tell, if anyone asked. Beth had just sat by at that time, allowing the men to sort out the disastrous situation they had been forced into. She really couldn't blame

Nothing ventured, nothing gained

Matthew about feeling the way he did about love. After all, it was love that had led the Mason family into adversity ten years ago.

Matthew paced up and down. His wide shoulders, long muscled back and handsome face tensed in concentration.. Matthew Mason was a man who could sweet talk himself into any business deal or out of one when the occasion arose. His smart mouth and quick brain had got him to where he was today, as a PR agent in his own league. Celebrities got their present agents to get Matthew's contact details, then sacked them as soon as they had the vital telephone number, which ensured a high-profile career from here on out. He had created some of the stars that people read about in *OK!* magazine. English, American, German or French, old or new, male or female, anyone who came to him got what they wanted: stardom. Matthew Mason was the man who made that happen. Of course, the women always wanted a bit more than their stardom, as Matthew was all muscle, smiles and hot libido. However, he also had the clever capability to tone down his looks and even act abashed at the attention he got. It drove the women wild if he acted innocent and vulnerable – or came on so strongly that the saying "bad boy" came to mind. Sadly (or not too sadly, as Matthew thought) in his thirty-one years a woman hadn't caught his attention to take him away from his work or make him be completely happy. He didn't think about the one woman who had nearly achieved this. Matthew had come to the conclusion that no perfect woman existed. He looked around his office. Indeed it was massive, scary and daunting, but the space came in handy when he was dealing with his female clients. Though he always mixed business with pleasure, he still had certain rules and made sure the women knew about them as well. But now his thoughts weren't on women, they were on his best friend Kevin. The phone call earlier had unsettled him and the urgency of Kevin's voice had made him anxious. However, he was also angry that Kevin should use the word "secret", especially in the way he did, as if he was proposing some sort of threat. Matthew didn't know if he was just messing around or meant something serious. Something told him it was the second option. How could his best friend even bring something like that up, he asked himself, how could he? Calm, he told himself, one, two, three. Matthew's arm swung out and hit the nearest lamp in an act of frustration. The lamp smashed against the wall and pieces of china flew at all directions.

"Damn," he said under his ragged breath. He strode across the room and opened the door violently, nearly knocking Tili off her feet. He barely looked at her as he walked past. In the gardens, breathing in the fresh, crisp spring air, he managed to calm himself down. He looked at the mansion. His mother and father had come across from Ireland ten years ago, buying this mansion and his father running his business from here. They were a wealthy family, dating from generations back, but had that rare quality of not

Nothing ventured, nothing gained

allowing the riches and money to go to their heads. Matthew had inherited his father's streak of arrogance, but it was only a part of his character and sometimes made him even more attractive to the opposite sex. To say Matthew used it to his advantage was an understatement. When his father had died three years ago from cancer, Matthew had moved his business up here to Hambledon, away from London, to be with his mother and help her manage the Maybrew estate. He preferred it to London as there he frequently got agitated by the crowds and public service. Hambledon suited him just fine. He liked the air, the space, the scenery, which was something to be enjoyed. The only thing wrong with this estate were the bloody horse footprints on the grounds. He would have to do something about that later.

Matthew strolled around the back garden, looking at the water feature his father had put in, the small baby angel standing on tip-toe, pursing its lips, where the water fell over the naked body of the stone. Lilies, pondweed and water spiders sat on top of the surface and below there were goldfish swimming excitedly around. Before him Matthew saw over five acres of land, all freshly cut, all glistening in the sun that had reappeared from behind the daunting clouds. The land rose slightly, and beyond that Matthew knew there were still six acres of the same grass. Furthermore there were two more acres afterwards, which they didn't mow or look after, as he and his mother had decided it was best to donate that as a public footpath to the council. They had enough land as it was. Matthew sighed, now at complete ease and smiling slightly as he thought about tomorrow's meeting. He and Kevin would sort out Kevin's problem, whatever it was, then they would get pissed, have a laugh and pull some really hot women. He laughed softly to himself as he made his way back to the entrance, and unbeknown to him, his mother's gaze followed his every step until he could no longer be seen.

Nothing ventured, nothing gained

Chapter three

Rosalie arrived at the cottage and found it in darkness.

"Damn!" she muttered, grabbing her coat and purse and running up the garden path. She was sure Donny would have let himself in; he knew where the spare key was hidden. She stepped into the hallway and saw the usual mess that she did every evening when she returned from Acorn stables. However, this time she tripped over a pile of suitcases, bags, carrier bags and a pile of clothes. Rosalie sighed: obviously he had found the key.

"Donny?" she called out and heard a movement upstairs. What the hell was he doing?

She went upstairs and was greeted with a new pile of clothes. She picked up a pair of trousers and a t-shirt. "Donny? Where the hell are you?" she yelled towards the empty rooms.

"Hey," came a voice from behind her.

Rosalie jumped back, her hand flying to her chest.

She saw Donny standing in the entrance to her bedroom, a towel draped across his hips, his arms loosely folded over his chest as he leant against the door frame.

"Christ, you are a bloody pain, you know that?" Rosalie said grumpily as she threw his trousers at him. "Put them back on and come downstairs."

"Jesus, this wasn't the type of greeting I expected," he replied, pouting.

"What greeting did you expect then?" Rosalie asked, hand on hip, looking at Donny's blue eyes staring mockingly back. He just smiled lazily and opened his arms as if offering something. Rosalie snorted, knowing damn well what he was doubtless ready to offer, and what she didn't want. No doubt in that, she told herself.

"You are getting a bed for the night and food in the morning," she said sternly. "That's it."

"What's got into you? You sounded happy when we talked earlier," Donny said as he dropped his towel and put his trousers on.

Rosalie averted her eyes. "Oh, just Lesley, Mary, Merlin."

"Merlin?" Donny asked.

"Yeah. The horse I love and who should be mine, the one I talk about all the time to you," Rosalie said sharply.

"Whoa! Yeah, I remember now." Donny picked up his used towel and folded it neatly.

"Well, I could buy it for you," he said, looking at her seriously.

Rosalie laughed, feeling some of her earlier good mood come back to life.

"Thank you, but he's not for sale."

"That's a pisser," he replied distractedly, looking for his shirt. Rosalie threw it at his face and they both began to laugh.

"That's what I like to hear. The wonderful laughter of Rosalie Rees." He looked at her, scanning his eyes up and down her body and ending with a low whistle. "You are looking hot, Lee," he said.

"Shut up!" she replied.

"Seriously. You've got that exotic look working for you. That skin, smooth and tempting, that long

Nothing ventured, nothing gained

brown hair." He whistled again. "Definitely complimentary."
"Piss off, Donny, I don't look any different to when you last saw me."
"No, I'm telling you and I swear on my stony, grey heart that you are definitely looking like something I could..."
"Be friends with?" she asked, laughing.
He shook his head. "You and I will never be friends, Lee. You know we're something else."
"You are seriously deluded. What did that Spanish heat do to you? Cook your brain?"
Donny laughed. "No, just made my skin look half as good as yours."
"Stop it," she said quietly, not sure she wanted to get into this conversation with Donny.
"You see, I can't," he replied, looking levelly into her brown eyes.
"How's dad?" she asked instead. Donny rolled his eyes, knowing what she was doing and allowing her to. For the time being.
"Your father tells me to say hello to you and Neus, and to give you a massive brown envelope." He looked around. "Which is downstairs."
"Great, another wad of cash to buy mine and Neus's love," she said as she followed Donny downstairs where he fished out the brown envelope.
"Where is Neus, anyway?"
"Modelling job in Paris. He left this morning."
"So this is an empty house?" he asked, looking up at Rosalie with a grin on his face.
"Yes. And you ruined my plans for this evening."

"Oh God, please don't tell me you were planning to satisfy yourself and I'm stopping you doing it? 'Cos I don't mind watching."
"You are disgusting and yes I was planning to satisfy myself..."
Donny groaned.
"But not in that way. I was planning to eat chocolate in my PJs and watch all the crappy soaps on TV."
"Oh damn! I was kind of hoping that it was the other satisfying technique."
"Can't you be serious?"
"I am."
"Jesus."
"Hey, I'm a man who has thought of no one else but you for the last two years."
"Yeah, me and the other woman who had the rugby husband."
"Lee, come on," he said as he tried to reach out for her. She moved away. "You are my sunshine, my only sunshine..."
"No! Anything but that!" Rosalie exclaimed, covering her ears.
Donny laughed and hugged her tightly. It was a joke between them that they had shared for the last six years, since they met. Donny had been on an assignment with Neus and it had been an advert to promote holiday deals. When Rosalie was introduced to Donny, the song had been playing in the background and they had joked about it. It was the first thing they had said to one another. Ever since, they both had shared a strange relationship of sex, friendship and

Nothing ventured, nothing gained

laughter. Whenever Donny came back to England after each assignment they would get together, as he was still a good friend of Neus's. It had been a long time since they had last shared their "special" meetings, because the last time Donny was in the country Rosalie had been seeing the writer of the postcard and she hadn't wanted to betray his trust, even though he had betrayed her trust every time he went home to his fiancée. Rosalie let her guard down for a moment as she felt the warmth of Donny's body seep through to hers. She needed a good hug from a good friend. The postcard had unsettled her, as had the woman called Tili crying earlier on. Although Rosalie hadn't wanted to think about it, she was sure Donny being home had unsettled her as well. She didn't want to resume their friendship; she wanted a purely Platonic one, without the sex.

Donny adjusted his body so he and Rosalie fitted better.

"Donny," she murmured, well aware of what he was trying to do.

"What?" he objected.

"Don't," she warned again.

"You're not still seeing him, are you?" he asked.

Rosalie sighed and breathed in Donny's smell. It was comforting and reassuring.

"No. But I got a postcard from him this morning."

"So, he went through with it?"

Silently Rosalie nodded, and again buried her face in Donny's neck, not caring if she permitted herself this luxury or not.

"I'm sorry to say I'm not sorry, Lee, you know how

I feel about you."

"Donny," she said, lifting her head to look into his eyes. "We're great friends and I don't want to lose you as one. But I don't want to pick up where we left off."

"But we're great together Lee, you know we are."

She shook her head. "I want to be serious. I want to have a boyfriend who I love and who is…. right for me."

"And that's not me?" Donny asked

Rosalie laughed. "You know it's not. You love sleeping around and hey, I can't blame you, but unfortunately I want my boyfriend to be faithful."

"I could be," Donny said, smiling slightly, trying to tease Rosalie out of her sadness.

"Maybe you will be, one day. But not now and not for me."

He shrugged. "If that's what you want but you know I love you," he said with a cheeky smile.

Rosalie laughed. "I love you too, Donny."

"Cool. Well, now that the no sex rule has been laid down I guess I'd better go," he said, then laughed as Rosalie's face changed and the anger showed in her eyes.

"Joking! Ow! Don't punch me!" Donny said, rubbing his arm.

"OK. I'll race you to change into your PJs and be in front of the TV with *Eastenders* on," Rosalie said.

"OK. Count of three. One, two... hey!" he exclaimed as Rosalie rushed into her own bedroom and shut the door.

Nothing ventured, nothing gained

The next morning, Rosalie felt much brighter. She went into the kitchen after taking a long bath and spending time on applying a light layer of make-up, and even brushing her hair this morning. Donny stopped chewing his piece of toast when he took in her appearance. His eyes roamed over her long, brown legs, looking incredible in white cotton shorts, and the black, sleeveless top complimenting her upper body.

"It's a shame you've gone celibate, 'cos I could really make you smile."

Rosalie looked over her shoulder and smiled at him. "There's no doubt in my mind that you could."

"So, what are you doing tonight?"

"Well…I've got this new job as a waitress at the Pitter Patter."

"Why? Do you need the money?"

"Yes, I'd like to have my own money. The cash you brought back with you from Dad, well…it's great but it's like guilt money. So, I'm just going to make my own way, like Neus does."

"What are you going to do about this?" Donny held up the postcard.

Rosalie's face changed to a bright pink and she lunged for it.

"Everything is great," Donny read from the postcard. "How are you? This is a great place to come for a honeymoon but I'm looking forward to getting home." Donny looked down at Rosalie's troubled face as he read. "Are you looking forward to it?" he asked, his eyebrow raised.

He looked at the card again. "Look after Merlin for Mary, you know how she gets anxious." Donny looked down at Rosalie again. "As I've told you before," he read. "Be back soon. I will phone you. Love Jack."

Rosalie covered her face and turned away from Donny.

"Wow, and he has signed it three kisses," he said sarcastically. "What a gracious man he is to allow you three kisses. Makes me sick."

Rosalie mumbled something beneath her hands and Donny had to step closer to hear it.

"What?"

"I said that I'm not planning to see him again."

"Yes, well, that's what you said before I left the last time. And in fact, that's what you always say to me after we sleep together. So how can I even begin to believe you?"

"Look, you're not my boyfriend, Donny, don't you judge me when you do worse than I've done," she snapped angrily, snatching the postcard out of his hands and throwing it in the bin.

"I've never received a postcard from a woman on her bloody honeymoon! That's an all-time low!" Donny shouted back at her.

"I didn't ask him to send me a postcard!"

"That's not the point and you know it."

"Jesus, you're acting as if I've betrayed you!"

"Well….." Donny turned angrily away and stalked out of the kitchen, slamming the door as he did. Rosalie retaliated by slamming the front door as she left to drive Ed to Acorn stables.

Matthew was not having a good day. There were mountains of paperwork on his desk, tons of

Nothing ventured, nothing gained

phone calls from his clients, a demanding current campaign going on, and Tili was being slow today, either deliberately or perhaps Matthew hadn't noticed how slowly she worked before. Then to top it all off, he was waiting in Pitter Patter for Kevin, who was fifteen minutes late. He thought back to the horrendous day he'd had. Too much work, too many clingy, self-loving clients and a lack of good workers to help him. To add to this, mother was acting rather strange. She had been asking him many questions about women, about what he planned to do in the future and what he would do with the estate when she died.

"Mother! Please don't talk about that," he had answered.

"I need to know for my own piece of mind, Matty."

"Well, I would keep it, of course. But let's not talk about morbid things."

"Nearly everything is morbid," his mother had replied, then walked out of the living room and went upstairs. Matthew wished he had more time to talk to Beth and enjoy her company, but work kept him so busy, and of course his mind was preoccupied with Kevin at the moment.

"I'm sorry, your waitress will be here any minute now," said the manageress, well aware that Matthew had been waiting to be served.

"Is there any other waiter?"

"I'm sorry. The restaurant is packed out; everyone is working their fingers to the bone."

"Yes, well, those who booked their table in advance should be priority," he snapped. The manageress walked away, trying to find someone else to serve that table. Matthew fiddled with his place mat, deep in thought.

"No, Ed! You are a freaking git for doing this to me!" Rosalie screamed at Ed's surrendering body on the side of the road. She was late on her first day! Why did Ed do this to her now? Janet was going to be as angry as hell. She hauled out her mobile phone and hoped Donny was in to save her.

"Matthew." Kevin greeted him with a warm tone and a brotherly hug.

"Kev, you look..."

"Shit," he finished for Matthew.

"Yeah, not too great. But how are you?"

"Oh, shit," he said with a laugh. "I could use a nice cold pint, though. Why haven't you ordered?"

"Our waitress is running late," Matthew answered with a shake of his head.

"Gives us time to talk then," Kevin said as he leant forward, hands crossed over the table.

Rosalie swore as she pulled the skirt over her hips, trying frantically to zip it up without getting the material caught. Her tights had laddered, showing a fair amount of leg, and her shirt had lost two buttons, revealing a sight of her black lacy bra. Rosalie was not having a good day. She eventually got the zip up and tucked the white blouse into it, only to look down and see a great big black stain on the green material.

"Damn," she said as she tried to rub it off with a wet paper towel in the ladies' toilet. It just smudged and made the stain look even worse.

Nothing ventured, nothing gained

How had Ed's oil gotten onto the green skirt?
"I'm not going to cry," she told herself as she turned her skirt around, so the stain was on her bum and the slit in the material was between her laddered legs. She looked into the mirror and cringed. Her brown hair had fallen out of its ponytail, looking messy and unkempt. Her face was red and blotchy and it was then she noticed that the black oil hadn't only got on her skirt, there was a massive streak of it down her left cheek.
She washed her face, making the streak worse and smudging her mascara at the same time.
"Lee! For Christ's sake!" Janet hissed from outside the bathroom door.
"I'm coming, Janet, just having an appearance problem."
"Fuck the appearance, just serve table five, they've been waiting an hour!"
Rosalie came out of the toilet and saw the look of horror across Janet's face.
"Lord, you have to clean up," Janet said as she pulled out all the paper towels and dabbed them over Rosalie's face.
"Mother Mary and her son Jesus, you can't go out like that."
"So, it's not 'fuck appearance' then?"
"Don't be a smart arse," Janet said as she wiped the blackness off Rosalie's face. They both looked into the mirror.
"It will have to do," Janet said as she pushed Rosalie out of the door.

"So, you expect her to stay at Maybrew Mansion?"

"Or somewhere else," Kevin answered

"This is ridiculous. My mother would think I got her pregnant. No, she'd have to stay somewhere else."

"Look Matt, wherever she stays, it's just got to be away from her father. He's not a nice man and she's..."

"Yes, in an arranged marriage. You've already gone through that bit." Matthew took a swig of beer from the bottle. "You're a prick."

Kevin nodded his head and looked up at his best friend's face wearing an apologetic look.

"I hate to do this to you, and your family, and I hate to have to bribe..."

"Blackmail," Matthew interrupted.

"No, I'm not."

"Then why bring my family into it?"

"To ensure you would do it. Because you wouldn't do it if I didn't. And don't say you would," he carried on as Matthew interrupted, "because your client's careers would be in danger. I get it, but that's why I have to use your family."

"This is too unreal."

"I'm a desperate man."

Matthew looked at him. "You must have been desperate to sleep with her. She's a complete dog."

"I was pissed and stoned," Kevin replied defensively.

"Robin Lotte? The only way she would get married would be arranged," Matthew continued, enjoying annoying Kevin. After all, his so-called best friend really had him tied down to help Robin Lotte when

Nothing ventured, nothing gained

he really didn't want to.

"Where will she stay?" Kevin asked.

"Bollocks," a voice said behind them. They both turned to see a woman re-adjusting her heels, after obviously tripping over them. Matthew looked at her. What a state, he thought, she should be fired. Kevin glanced her up and down appreciatively, even though she did look a mess. The woman turned around, appearing lost and scared. She spotted Matthew and Kevin looking at her and consulted her notepad. Matthew could have sworn he saw her cringe when she looked at the table number. She walked up, trying to hold her head high and smiled at them both.

"Hey guys, sorry about the wait. Bloody car broke down."

Kevin laughed, but Matthew just stared at her.

"Do you want to order now or want some more drinks?" she asked sweetly.

"What's your name, honey?" Kevin asked, smiling.

Matthew rolled his eyes. He looked back to the woman, who had caught him rolling his eyes, and smiled.

"I'm Rosalie."

"That's a nice name."

"I hate it," she replied to Kevin, still looking at Matthew. Inside, Rosalie's heart was thumping. This man was a looker!

"Well, Rosalie, can I have the duck and Matt, what do you want?"

"I'll have the..." he consulted his menu. "Loin steak."

"OK, cool," Rosalie said as she made to go.

"And," Matthew said pointedly, looking at her with obvious disgust in his eyes, "I want it well done, with all the extra garnishes. I'm very hungry."

"Yes, I can imagine, again I'm sorry about that."

"Perhaps another bottle of wine, but not the watered-down one brought to us earlier. We'll have the Lindeman's Merlot 2003. I assume you know which one that is?" he asked, looking at Rosalie.

Forget looker, she thought, try arsehole.

"Sure," she said.

"Are you going to write it down?" Matthew asked.

"I have a good memory," Rosalie replied quickly.

He looked into her eyes.

"Is that so? Doesn't seem you remembered that the image of a waiter represents the restaurant."

"Waitress," corrected Rosalie, "and it doesn't seem that you have a good memory either."

"How's that?"

"Just that, you don't remember that regardless of what occupation someone has, everyone is equal."

"I find that hard to believe."

"How so, Matt?" she asked, remembering the other man calling him that earlier.

Matthew narrowed his eyes. "You really should try working on your people skills," he said instead of an answer to her question.

"My people skills are fine. I have other skills that need to be tested out."

"What other skills?"

"I'm not saying for people who clearly are not worth my people skills."

Nothing ventured, nothing gained

"Hah!"

"What 'hah'?" Rosalie asked, eyes still holding his direct stare. Brown eyes challenging brown eyes.

"The way you are presented, even tramps deserve your people skills."

"Matt mate, come on, you're being really rude," Kevin said, smiling apologetically at Rosalie.

"I'm sure it's out of Matt's character to be this rude. Especially to a waitress on her first day, who genuinely feels bad about being late," she said to Kevin, even though she still looked directly at Matthew, who just stared back at her.

He knew he was being unfair and should apologise to her, but he'd just been put into a situation which he had no control over and which was, quite frankly, a pain. His best friend was using the one secret he had trusted him to keep against him, to blackmail him into helping him. Matthew thought it was a great betrayal and was hurt that Kevin could do such a thing. It also annoyed him that Kevin didn't think that he would help him just out of friendship, without having a hold over him. Rosalie saw that the argument wasn't the thing that Matt was thinking about any more. He was good-looking, sure, but arrogant and bloody rude. She didn't need him as a customer, but a job is a job, she told herself, even though she'd love to disfigure that annoyingly handsome, smug face.

"I'll put your order in with the chef and come back with your wine," she said before she left the table, but not before she heard the other man say to Matt: "Why the hell were you so rude to her?"

"Because you've made me fucking angry," she heard him reply before going into the kitchen. Kevin looked at Matt, the guilt evident in his expression. "I know," he said before covering his face. "I'm sorry, if there were someone else who could help me..."
"It's not helping you, you idiot, it's the way you're making me help you."
"I'm sorry."
"Fuck, sorry. I trusted you with my biggest secret."

Rosalie heard the last bit as she brought the wine over. Instantly both men went quiet while she opened it. She gritted her teeth when she got the foil caught up in the wine opener. "Balls!" she muttered, then clasped her hand over her mouth, looking at both men. But then she noted that they weren't looking at her, they were looking at the bottle swinging from side to side and toppling over onto the floor, where a massive smash erupted. The other diners looked at her for a moment, and then returned to their mutterings and food. Kevin laughed in a comforting way, but Matthew just looked at her, shaking his head.
"Twat," she said under her breath as she began the task of picking up the glass.
"Excuse me?" asked that sexy, yet arrogant, self-righteous voice.
She looked up sucking her finger as she'd nicked it on a piece of glass.
Matthew stared down at her, feeling guilty for his rudeness earlier, but also feeling pity for her as she was making such a pig's ear of serving them.

Nothing ventured, nothing gained

"Nothing," he said as he turned back to face Kevin.
"Don't offer to help," Rosalie said under her breath.
"Do you always mutter under your breath?" he asked, turning back to her.
"Yes," she smiled sweetly at him. "It preserves my oxygen."
"I can tell you don't like to waste your breath," he said.
"Well, you clearly don't mind wasting yours on sarcasm."
"Better to waste it on something that makes a point," he answered and smiled.
Rosalie would have come up with a snappish reply, if it hadn't been for that smile. So arrogant, but his perfect set of teeth, dimples in his cheeks, laughter lines appearing under his eyes meant she had her own eyes transfixed on his face. Damn him for having good looks, she thought. She got up and walked away to get the dustpan and brush. As she knelt down she could feel her tights ladder even further up her thigh.

After serving the wrong dishes to the wrong tables, spilling drinks on the tablecloths, bringing extra forks instead of knives, and charging too much on the bills, Rosalie was exhausted by the time she went to table number five to give them the bill.
"Here we go," she said as she placed it down.
Matthew got out his credit card, but Kevin stopped him.

"It's the least I can do", he said as he placed it down on the table.

Interesting, thought Rosalie.

She cashed the bill up, printed out the receipt, and made her way back over to the table.

"Thank you for coming to Pitter Patter, please do come again," she said in a flat voice. She was dog-tired and pissed off that this evening hadn't gone well.

"I don't think that's a possibility," Matthew said as he put on his coat. Rosalie was about to say something back, but then shut her mouth and tried to bite back the tears that were swelling up in her eyes. She glanced back up to bid them goodnight, but locked eyes with those brown ones again. She didn't want him to see that she was on the verge of tears, so she looked away and smiled at Kevin, saying "Drive safe" before walking away to safely release her anger in the form of salty droplets.

Nothing ventured, nothing gained

Chapter four

Those brown eyes haunted him. The shiny glaze they had over them, the brightness and vulnerability they had suddenly shown. Since that evening he had felt guilty at the unreasonable way he had behaved towards her at the restaurant. Yet those eyes had held a strong power, a self-power and a sense of inner strength all throughout the evening, even when they both had been passing snappish retorts to each other. Matthew didn't think he fancied her, but he definitely liked the way she handled herself. It had been a week since that evening. It was Sunday today, Matthew's only day off from work, and even then he worked from his bedroom or in the lounge. Just not in his office. He had looked into searching for houses for Robin, but it was just bad luck that nothing was available in Kevin's price range. As a carpenter, some months were better than others, so Kevin had put a limit down and so far, every available house had exceeded that limit. Matthew knew he could help Kevin out with his money situation, but Matthew's pride stopped him. He wouldn't help the man who was blackmailing him into helping him. It just irritated him beyond belief that someone else was pulling his puppet strings. Last night, to relieve some tension, he had gone out with his client, Miranda Wilson, the sports model. She was a gorgeous woman with a great body, but all he saw were those brown eyes looking at him with amusement and anger, like they had done during the evening. As soon as he could, he pushed

Miranda out of his bed and into the taxi that was waiting to drive her back home. He then thought about why he kept seeing those brown eyes and came to the conclusion that he was feeling guilty for treating her so badly. He would go to the restaurant in an hour, as it was eleven already, and apologise. This would surely get her out of his system.

Rosalie was at the Acorn stables, happily mucking out Merlin's stable, when Mary and Jack Blindle walked up the yard towards her, hand in hand. Paul McCartney was singing about "Rocky Racoon" when she finally closed her gawping mouth and shut the stable door without being seen by Jack and Mary. They had, thankfully, been stopped by Lesley, who must have somehow sensed Rosalie's shock. She carried on mucking out as if she hadn't noticed them, and hoped they hadn't seen her. No such luck. Someone tapped her shoulder and she turned to see Mary and Jack. Rosalie quickly tugged the earphones out of her ears and wiped her head free of sweat. It was a perfect May day: the sun was shining, the birds singing and everyone in good spirits. And now it was all ruined.
"Hi!" Rosalie said a bit too falsely and brightly.
"Hello, Rose," Mary answered. Rosalie didn't look at Jack and just continued smiling at Mary as she talked.
"Good holiday?"
"Yes. It was wonderful, the perfect honeymoon, wasn't it, Jack?" Mary turned to her new husband.

Nothing ventured, nothing gained

Even though Mary was looking at Jack, Rosalie continued to look at Mary, studying her face. She noted that she had a mole on her neck. She could feel Jack's stare on her, but refused to look at him.
"It was great," she heard that familiar voice say.
"Great!" Rosalie exclaimed.
Mary turned back to her. "How's Merlin?"
"Oh, he's great. I was just going to get him in and tack him up for a ride," Rosalie said brightly.
"Ah, right, well I was going to leave this till later, but I'll tell you now," Mary said.
"I'm attending a horse event in July. And I will need to have Merlin to practise my dressage and show jumping for the competition."
Rosalie's mouth hung open again, her face went pale and she didn't know what to say.
"Of course, you can still have a few Sundays to ride him, but basically, your time with him will be cut down considerably."
Paul McCartney was singing about "Yesterday" as Rosalie tried to think of what to say.
"So…" her voice broke. "Um, so you are going to compete with Merlin?" Rosalie hadn't meant for it come out as high as it had.
"Yes. I'm going to do a novice dressage test and the 3 foot jumping."
"3 foot?"
"Yes," Mary said with unmistakable impatience.
"You are welcome to watch," Jack said.
Suddenly Rosalie's eyes snapped to his face and their eyes locked. She could have sworn she saw him back down from her gaze.
"Right," Rosalie said, gathering her wits. "Well, I'm

going to get Merlin and ride him now. I'll see you tomorrow." She shot one last look at Jack which summed up how she felt about him and smiled at Mary. Rosalie grabbed the saddle and bridle by Jack's side and knocked him back with it. "Sorry," she said to him, but before he answered, she strode off towards Merlin's field.

Matthew wandered the Maybrew gardens. They had told him that she wasn't on today's shift and wouldn't be until next Friday. Next Friday! He thought. I can't have my sex life messed up until next Friday. He'd asked for her home address or number, but the snotty manager called Janet had refused. He was about to turn back and walk the two acres when he saw something shiny catch the sunlight. He looked closer and swore when he saw another horse and rider on his grounds. He was going to let the rider have the full brunt of his frustration. Rosalie jumped off Merlin with a burst of energy she didn't feel. She stoked Merlin's neck and laughed when she saw the dopey-eyed look he gave her.
"I love you, boy," she said to him, then tied the reins and allowed him to graze on the nice patch of grass she'd found. Thankfully they were in the shade so she could sit down and take a breather. She'd had a bad week. Donny had left a few days after her first day at the restaurant, telling her that she needed to find that boyfriend otherwise he'd be back with a vengeance. She had laughed, but knew it wasn't funny. Donny's feelings about Jack were strong, and strange, she thought,

Nothing ventured, nothing gained

considering he slept with engaged females or even married ones all the time. Then of course the guy at the restaurant, the arrogant, but oh-so-good-looking git. Rosalie referred to him as "the good-looking git" nowadays since it summed up her feelings about him perfectly. She had tried to ignore the fact that he had been in her thoughts this week, she told herself it was her anger welling up each time she thought of him. Now Jack and Mary were back, looking loved-up and happy, which wasn't what pissed Rosalie off, it was the fact that Mary was competing Merlin this summer. Dressage! Show jumping! Rosalie snorted. If Merlin weren't such a willing horse, Mary would have sold him ages ago. It was the magic of Merlin that made Mary Blindle look good when she was on top of him. If only Mary suddenly decided to sell Merlin, Rosalie thought. She didn't know how she'd afford to keep him, but she'd find a way.
"Look, I've told your stable many times before," a strangely familiar voice said to the side of her. She turned around and was surprised to find herself looking at the good-looking git.
Matthew took a step back, surprised to see those brown eyes look into his, surprised to see her at all on his grounds. Neither of them spoke.
Merlin snorted and began to dig a hole in the grass, demanding attention.
"Hi," Matthew said, snapping himself out of his dumbstruck and shocked state.
"Hey," Rosalie answered, slightly anxious and worried.

Once again there was silence.
"What are you doing here?" they both asked in unison.
"I'm riding," Rosalie said, stating the obvious.
"I can see that. Why are you riding on my land?"
"Jeez, this is *your* land?"
"Yes."
"Oh."
"So, what are you doing on it?"
"I told you, I'm riding."
"And I've told your yard many times, that it is trespassing."
"And *I'm* telling you that unless you get something official written up, then I won't take any notice."
"I could have you arrested."
"Go ahead," Rosalie said, folding her wrists together.
Matthew sighed and raked a hand through his hair. "You think I won't?"
"I think you will," Rosalie answered, smiling.
Damn! Those brown eyes started to sparkle at him. He went quiet for a while and looked at the big horse staring at him, as if warning him away from his mistress.
"That horse looks as though he's about to kill me," Matthew said instead.
Rosalie looked at Merlin and smiled fondly. "He's very protective."
"Hmm, like a father to his daughter?"
"Well…I guess, but he's certainly not my father," Rosalie said.
Matthew looked at her and knew she was mocking him. "Could have fooled me", he answered.

Nothing ventured, nothing gained

"Excuse me?"
"What?"
"Are you implying that I look like a horse?" Rosalie said; hand on hip, narrowing her eyes slightly.
Matthew burst out laughing with genuine amusement. He hadn't meant anything of the sort, but the fact that she had drawn that conclusion from his remark was funny. After a while, he realised that Rosalie was laughing with him, and that made him laugh even more. It felt good that the tension was broken.
"So, this is your horse?" Matthew asked, going towards Merlin attentively.
"He won't hurt you, and no, he isn't my horse."
Matthew frowned at her. "Then why are you riding it?"
"Him," she corrected. "Because I work all week at Acorn stables to enjoy this ride every Sunday."
Matthew took the final step towards Merlin and jumped back as the horse lunged for him.
"That animal is dangerous," Matthew said.
Rosalie went to Merlin and patted his neck.
Matthew swore he saw the look of triumph in Merlin's dopey, black eyes.
"He doesn't take well to strangers," Rosalie said as she looked back at Matthew.
"Yeah, like his rider," Matthew muttered.
"I thought you didn't believe in wasting breath," Rosalie said when she heard him mutter something.
He looked up sharply, remembering their conversation. They stared at each other, once again brown eyes on brown eyes, and then

Matthew smiled.
"Yeah. Sorry about the other week," he said.
Rosalie couldn't have been more surprised if he'd turned around and announced his undying love for her.
"I was in a shitty mood and I took it out on you. You see, my friend just told me about something I have….Well, I'm sorry." He shrugged.
Rosalie smiled gently. "Thank you. I'm sorry that I wasn't professional, I had just had the day from hell."
"So, are you continuing with the job?" he asked.
"Sure. I never quit the first time." She smiled, and then went to sit on the tree trunk she had been on earlier. Matthew followed and sat next to her. She glanced at the space between them. Good, keep the distance, she thought, although she felt a strange sense of disappointment.
"So, you live here?" she asked.
"Yeah. My parents and I moved here ten years ago."
"Was the mansion in your family or did you buy it?"
"We bought it."
"Cool."
They were both silent.
"Where do you live?"
"Harpsden."
"Family?"
"Sure, I've got my brother Neus."
"Neus?"
"What about him?" she asked, eyes dangerously narrowed.

Nothing ventured, nothing gained

"That's a Spanish name, isn't it?"
"Yeah."
"And your name is Rosalie."
"Well done. Now what colour is the sky?" she asked with a smile.
Matthew rolled his eyes at her childish behaviour, even though he found it funny.
"Well, you've got a pretty English name and Neus has a Spanish name, how come?" Rosalie tried not to let her mind concentrate on the fact that he'd called her name pretty.
"My mother was English, my father Spanish. They flipped a coin on which child to give an English name and the other a Spanish."
"Oh, I see."
"Do you have a brother or sister?" she asked.
"No." Matthew shook his head.
"Do you regret that?"
He looked up and their brown eyes locked together. "No," he said.
"These grounds are pretty," Rosalie said, breaking their stare and looking around her.
"Yes they are. In the summer they are even better."
"I can't believe you're the man who has been giving us so much grief about riding."
"And I can't believe you are one of those riders who annoy the hell out of me and my mother."
"Tili?" Rosalie asked.
"Do you know her?"
"Just in the same way you and I met." Rosalie smiled at him as she saw him trying to work it out and saw the realisation dawn in his brown eyes.

"You're the person who made her cry?" he asked, his voice high with disbelief.
"I didn't mean to," she replied defensively.
"Do you go around having a go at everyone?" he asked.
"Excuse me?"
"You had a go at me the first time we met and then poor Tili."
"Tili was acting like you when she spoke to me, arrogant and rude."
"So, you made her cry?" Matthew's voice was flat.
"She's just…wet."
"Don't talk about her like that."
"Hit a nerve, have I?" Rosalie teased as she got up and walked over to Merlin.
"Course not. But she is young and loyal."
"You make her sound like a dog."
"Yeah, well, she's been following me around everywhere," he said with a grin.
"Puh-lease."
"It's the truth."
"Uh-huh."
Rosalie mounted Merlin and gathered her reins.
"You know, you could ride me instead of that horse," Matthew offered, his cheeky grin on his face and the mischievous look in his brown eyes.
Rosalie looked doubtful. "You won't be riding anything if you keep that up."
"Don't be too sure."
"You know, your arrogance isn't attractive."
"I think it is." he stepped closer to Rosalie and Merlin, who obediently took a step back with Rosalie's instruction.

Nothing ventured, nothing gained

"Take it from a woman who deals with arrogant people all the time."
"You didn't handle me very well."
"Yeah, well, you were so unbelievably rude."
"I have apologised."
"And said it in your arrogant, condescending tone. It wasn't believable."
"So what can I do then?"
"Take a hike?" she asked nicely, then spurred Merlin in the stomach and they galloped off, leaving a smiling Matthew behind.

Chapter five

Neus opened the front door and yelled out for Rosalie. There was no answer as he managed to manhandle himself and all his suitcases, plus extra ones full of clothes he was to keep, through the door. He heaved one last sigh as he pulled the metal one through the width of the door, scraping the side paint. He and Lee really had to redecorate the cottage and make it more homely, he decided, as he shut the front door and Rosalie walked through to the hallway.

"Neus!" she exclaimed, giving him a hug.

"Hey little Lee, how are you?" he asked, hugging her back.

"A lot has happened since you went away."

"Like what?" he asked, taking his jacket off and putting it on the banister.

"Oh, Jack is back, Merlin is going to be competed by Mary, Donny came back for a few days and I have met the most arrogant, annoying, sexy, good-looking man."

"Wow, a lot has happened. So take me through it, step by step."

They both sat down and began eating biscuits as Rosalie told him about Jack's postcard, Mary's horse show, Donny's attempts to sleep with her, and finally Matthew. As he sat there listening, Neus decided that he hadn't seen his sister this happy or have as much energy for a long time. Whoever this Matthew guy was, he liked him immediately.

"How's your love life?" Rosalie asked, reaching for

Nothing ventured, nothing gained

another chocolate biscuit.

Neus sighed. "I'm bored of the usual shit. There are tons of models, but….they're so painfully skinny. I like to have something to grab, you know?"

"Yeah. Well, that's what I tell myself men want when I eat crisps and chocolate," Rosalie said with a smile.

"But it's bloody true. I don't want skin and bones with nothing but ear wax between their ears."

Rosalie grimaced.

"Lee, I want someone who's... normal." Neus dropped his head into his hands and Rosalie looked at him, eyes narrowed, trying to figure out what had happened to him on this trip to make him come to this conclusion.

"You've always been happy with models before," she said carefully.

"I'm twenty-six, I'm not a spring chicken any more."

"You're hardly old," Rosalie interrupted.

"Yeah, but getting older by the second. I want someone who… likes me for me, not because of my looks and great body."

"God, got an ego?" she laughed.

"This is serious," he replied with a scowl.

There was a knock at the door and Gwen Baxter walked in carrying a washing basket. She placed it down on the side, before joining Rosalie and Neus at the table.

"Rose, I've got your washing there," she said while pinching a biscuit. "But I haven't done yours, Neus, I wasn't sure when you'd be back."

"That's OK, Gwen."
"What's wrong, chicken?" she asked.
Neus began to tell the whole story to Gwen, who sat listening intently. Rosalie watched Gwen's face and reactions. The comforting gestures, such as a hand over his, a smile when he looked up, a shake of her head when he described the floozy models and just her company and presence. Rosalie was so glad that Gwen was around, but at the age of seventy, Neus and Rosalie had to face the fact that Gwen may need looking after soon instead of her looking after them all the time. But Rosalie decided that they shouldn't worry, as Gwen always looked as alive as ever, bursting with energy, always around for a gossip and lending a hand when needed. Rosalie concentrated on her grey hair, so thick and curly, cut into a bob. Her blue eyes sparkled when she talked and her lips curved in a smile when she was happy. There was an aura that followed her around, so happy, alive and alert, as if expecting the next chapter in her life. This made Rosalie and Neus feel safe, as her aura indicated that she had a long, everlasting journey that had merely begun.
"Well, chicken, just keep searching. I tell you what, I know this woman, well…she's a bit of an old bag really."
Rosalie and Neus looked at each other, smiling.
"But apparently, she has a nice granddaughter, about your age I'd say. Want me to set something up?"
Neus smiled kindly at Gwen, but shook his head. "No, I need to find her on my own. Excuse me for

Nothing ventured, nothing gained

a minute, I'm gonna unpack, then we can all sit down and gossip."
"Sorry, I've got to get back to the stables," Rosalie said, jumping up.
"It's your lunch," Gwen pointed out.
"Yeah, but the sooner I get done, the sooner I can get home and change for Pitter Patter, then I can be more prepared for snotty customers."
"So, it's not just the fact that Matthew might have called at the stables?" Gwen asked. Rosalie narrowed her eyes. "It isn't, actually."
"And the fact that you have those barely there shorts and mini tank top that shows off you belly button, that has nothing to do with him either?" Neus asked, joining in and enjoying his sister's discomfort.
"No, it's hot outside."
"Uh-huh. And the fact that you've been looking at your mobile for messages means nothing either?"
"That's right. He doesn't have my mobile number," she said, getting her jumper and bag together.
"And was I mistaken that I heard you earlier talking to Lesley, telling her your number in case anyone calls around for you?"
Gwen sat back in her chair and Neus stood behind her. To Rosalie, they both had the look of a smart-arsed politician, eyebrows raised and that knowing look in their eyes.
"That was in case Mary needed me for Merlin," Rosalie lied.
"Lee, do you think he would come and look for you?"
Was it just Rosalie, or did she sense that they

both didn't believe her about Matthew?
"He may not. Either way, I don't care. I've got two jobs on the go, Ed is in the dog house and I'm walking all the way to Henley then getting a bus to the stables, so he's the last thing on my mind."
Gwen nodded, as if to end the conversation, then she smiled at them both. "I've got a favour to ask," she said.
"Anything," Neus said.
"You see, my friend has gone out of the country for a few months and she asked me to look after this dog. Now, I'm not really a dog lover you see, so I was wondering if..."
"Sure. We'd love to," Rosalie interrupted, her brown eyes shining in excitement.
Neus looked at Gwen and smiled. "Lee always wanted a dog when she was younger, but because we travelled a lot, we obviously couldn't."
"We could have, if mum and dad really wanted me to be happy," Rosalie said, rolling her eyes.
"So, is it OK then?" Gwen asked again.
"Ok? It's bloody great! What's its name? Boy or girl? And what breed?"
Gwen's mind boggled at the questions. She hadn't really been listening to her friend Marjorie when she'd gone into detail about the dog.
"Well, it's next door in my cottage now if you..."
But before she could finish her sentence, Rosalie had rushed out towards Gwen's cottage.
"Sorry Gwen, you know our Lee, she's a big animal lover, whether it's snakes and spiders, to puppies and kittens."
"I'm glad she likes animals. Never trust anyone

Nothing ventured, nothing gained

who hates animals."
"I thought you didn't like animals."
"I'm not *fond* of dogs, but I love goldfish."
Neus laughed. Rosalie walked back in carrying a very scared-looking King Charles spaniel, with big floppy ears and a long brown and white coat. Rosalie looked into its scared eyes and stroked its head. She thought she saw a flicker of trust for a moment, but then the fright returned to the dog's eyes.
"It's a boy. What's his name?" Rosalie asked.
"Sucker."
"Sucker?" Rosalie asked.
"Something about sucking all his mother's milk without leaving any for his brothers and sisters, I don't know. Marjorie has another dog called Splitter, I assume because it split things in half…"
Rosalie looked down into Sucker's eyes and smiled again. "I'll walk him to the stables, then let him wander around, you know, get a feel for me."
"OK. I'll bring Sucker's stuff over later. Now I must dash, I've got an appointment to sew Mrs Subway's dress back together. Honestly, why does she buy things too small?"
"People like to have something tight on them," Neus said with a shrug.
"Hah!" Rosalie exclaimed, letting Sucker down and snapping his lead on. "See you guys later," she said as she and Sucker left.
Neus and Gwen watched her go. "If I didn't know my own sister, I'd say she was in love."
"She isn't yet, Neus, but she is already halfway down that road," Gwen said, with a secret smile.

Beth Mason looked down at her son sitting in his massive chair; a telephone plastered to his head, and wondered what change had taken place. He almost seemed...happy to talk about his life now. Just a week ago, when she had brought up the subject of a possible wife, he had snapped her head off. In fact, now she thought about it, when he had come home after his Sunday walk, he had been so much more cheerful. Beth shook her head. He was always upbeat after walking around the Maybrew gardens, a luxury that he hardly had time for. Unlike Beth, who always strolled around the fields and picked apples and berries from the jungle, she and her husband had grown. Although now was not the time to be wistful, she told herself. The news she'd heard was shocking, then when Matthew's name had been mentioned she thought the news was damn untrue, or at least she hoped it was.

Matthew put the phone down and smiled up at his mother. She looked anxious, as if about to tell him something, but scared of how she'd say it or how he would take it. He hoped it wasn't another talk about a wife, he didn't want to get married and he thought he had made that perfectly clear to his mother. Yet he had to admit he had caught himself looking into the future this past week, but it wasn't one of his mother's women who was playing his wife in his fantasies.
"Mother," he said warmly.
"Matthew." She nodded.

Nothing ventured, nothing gained

"What's up?"

"Well...I've heard news. And very disagreeable I think, but I need an honest answer."

"OK," he replied, unsure.

"Have you got Robin Lotte pregnant?" There was a stunned silence from Matthew.

He didn't know how to answer that question. If he said yes, then he'd have to admit to sleeping with Robin Lotte, heaven forbid! But if he said no, then he'd have to admit Kevin's blackmail of his family, which would no doubt cause his mother unnecessary stress.

While Matthew was debating his answer, the silence between them confirmed Beth's worst nightmares.

"Oh, you stupid little boy!" she exploded, slapping him across the cheek. Matthew winced as the sting settled in.

"How could you? Do you have any idea that she's promised to someone else? That she's heiress to Lord Kurt's estate and empire?"

"Yes, but I didn't..."

"Do not make excuses for your stupid actions!"

"Mother, it isn't me who got..."

"Fool!" Beth shouted again, getting mixed up with her anger and sadness.

"For Christ's sake mother, listen!" Matthew shouted, standing up.

"Say what you have to say, and then go," she ordered.

"Mother, Kevin got Robin pregnant, I didn't. I haven't even met her!"

Beth looked confused. "Then why is your name

involved with hers?"

"Because I'm helping Kevin find her a place to stay."

"Why can't Kevin do it on his own?"

Matthew sighed and sat down in his chair again, running a hand through his black hair.

"Because he's an idiot, and he came to me because I'm his friend."

"You do not need to help him."

"He is my best friend and he knows everything about me and you and dad, and…" His words trailed off as his mother held up her hand, signalling that she'd got what he was trying to say.

"I do not like the fact that you will be helping her run away from her father. Good Lord! If Kurt got wind of this…."

"I don't want to do it either, but it's the only way."

Beth paced Mathew's office as she thought of what to do. "Have you got any other trustworthy friends?" she asked.

"None that could deal with a secret like this," he answered.

"John?" she asked.

"What? John Beker?"

"Yes," she said.

"No way! He'd try to seduce her."

"Robin isn't a very pretty woman," she pointed out.

"I know," he said.

Beth threw him a dirty look. "Do you have a girlfriend who could help out?"

Matthew narrowed his eyes at his mother. "You mean, you're trying to find out my marital status as well as solve this problem?"

Nothing ventured, nothing gained

"I am your mother, I deserve to know."

"Well, at the moment I'm not doing anything with anyone."

Beth continued pacing. "Maybe if we pretend she's a distant cousin."

"I think they'd find out we are not related to Lord Kurt."

"No, I meant to one of your girlfriends."

"Have you just heard what I said? I have NO girlfriend."

"You have your father's genes; of course you have a girlfriend. When I met him he had at least five on the go."

"Mother!"

"Fine. Well, I find that hard to believe. You're a smart, handsome man, with a lot of money and this mansion."

"It's technically your mansion."

"I won't be around for ever," Beth said, looking at him seriously. "I want someone to look after you, Matthew."

"Mother, please let's get back onto the subject matter."

"Fine. But this conversation isn't over."

What Beth had said unsettled Matthew. He'd always assumed his mother would be around for ever, and now she was saying she wouldn't be. Did she know something about her health and wasn't telling him? Or was she just merely being organised for when the time did come? Matthew didn't know, and he didn't have to time to find out at the moment.

"We need a woman who can keep a good secret

and be willing to help us out. Of course, we need to give something in return. Perhaps money?" Beth asked. Matthew nodded and thought, his mind ticking over. A woman who needed something from them, but who could keep a secret…

Suddenly, the answer came to him. "Or, a woman who has an interest in our land," he said to his mother, with a grin.

"We Will Rock You" drummed into Rosalie's ear, loudly. "Waving your banner all over the place…," sang Rosalie in an off-beat tone. "Rock you!" she exclaimed, locking the stable door behind her and wheeling her wheelbarrow over to the muck heap. Brian May's guitar solo came on and it was all she could do not to grab the fork and pretend it was her guitar. She looked around and noticed no one was there, so she thought, what the hell! She grabbed the fork and began twiddling her fingers, bending over in an exaggerated pose, swaying her head from side to side so her brown hair fell in front of her face. "Yeah! We will, we will ROCK you!" she bellowed, momentarily forgetting where she was and thinking she was in the safety of her own bedroom. Ever since she was a little girl, Rosalie had had a massive passion for music. Her father's taste in Spanish music had prompted her to listen, but she didn't take to that type of music. It was when her mother gave her her first Beatles album that she had enjoyed their melodies, especially their earlier sounds from the

Nothing ventured, nothing gained

sixties. From then on Rosalie had listened to all types of music, forming her own opinion of each song. She liked a large variety of different music, but had a soft spot for rock. Brian May finished his guitar solo and she knew the next song on her play list was "Charmless Man" by Blur.
"I met him...." She trailed off, suddenly being jolted back to reality and taking in her situation. She was leaning over a fork on top of the muck heap, singing to herself, and Jack was watching her from the bottom.
"We need to talk," he said quietly.
"Sure," Rosalie said, embarrassed and thankful he didn't pass a comment. She climbed down slowly, trying not to trip, and made it to the bottom where she faced him, eyebrows raised in a questioning way.
"Did you get my postcard?" he asked, stepping closer to her.
"No," she lied, taking a step back.
"Oh. Well, I sent you one, saying I was having a good time and that I was looking forward to coming back."
"That's nice," she replied coldly.
"Shit, Lee, how can you be this cool when you can feel the heat between us?" he asked, a smug smile lighting his fake green contacts. She'd always hated those green contacts, she much preferred to see the real colour of his eyes, but he was so vain he thought green complimented his hair better.
"There's heat, but it's being caused from you burning in hell."

"Burn," he said huskily, his voice dropping lower, "burn with me in sin."

"No thanks, your sins are not my problem any more," she said as she made to go, but he wrapped an arm around her waist and pulled in front of him again.

"You seemed to love to help me sin, you seemed to BEG for me to sin with you." Rosalie dropped her head in shame. It was true, she had been a sucker for all his charm and she had been blinded by love and lust. But now she had seen Jack for what he was: a vain, rude, disrespectful arsehole. And that was only some of the names she'd created for him.

"That was when I didn't think I had a chance in heaven. I do now."

"What do you mean?" His smug smile dropped slightly.

Rosalie panicked. She hadn't meant anything by it, but decided it was better to go that way if it stumped his arrogant nature. Jeez, she thought, and I reckoned Matt was arrogant. Matt is a freaking saint compared to this idiot.

"I feel needed, I feel as if I'm worth something. So go sin with someone else, because I'm praying in heaven with someone else."

"You mean you're shagging someone else."

"Nicely put, Jack."

"Cut to the point." His voice had turned harsh, his smile had gone and his eyes were cold.

"Basically, I saw through you."

"Yeah, like you've seen inside me, the outside of me, in fact you said you loved all of me."

Nothing ventured, nothing gained

"That was before I met my....angel." God! How corny could she get?
"Angel?" Jack asked, obviously finding her amusing.
"Yeah. My....saviour." Rosalie, stop now, stop now....
"And you like your saviour better than your sinner?"
"Yes."
Jack looked around them and then pulled her towards him and planted a solid kiss flat on her closed lips. His hand roamed under her tank top and began to feel the outline of her lacy bra. Push him off, she screamed at herself. Kick him in the balls, scratch his fake green eyes out, anything! Rosalie opened her eyes and looked back into Jack's, his hand playing with her belly piercing now, twisting it around, up and down as he continued to kiss her. Rosalie kept her mouth tightly shut, so he wouldn't go any further than she permitted, then grabbed his wandering hand, pushed it away and gave him a punch to his chest, in an attempt to get him off her. He merely laughed as he stumbled a few feet back and stood there smiling at her. She wiped her mouth with the back of her hand and spat on the concrete.
"If you do that again, I will personally remove what you use to sin with."
"I felt it though, didn't you?"
"Felt what?" she asked, sighing.
"The desire, the attraction and the passion," he whispered, moving towards her again.
She moved past him, walking with deliberate pace

to get away from him. No such luck though, as he caught up with her and tugged her arm.

"Come on, Lee, you know we're made for each other."

"Of course we are. That's why you decided to marry someone else. Because you know I'm your soul mate."

"Don't do this, don't fight it."

"Fuck you!" she exploded, her patience gone and her anger flaring. "How low can you seriously go? You send me a postcard on your honeymoon, what type of game is that? What about Mary? Christ, does she know what a slime ball she's married? I guess not, because when you're with her you're the caring, loving, husband her daddy paid for." Rosalie stopped to get her breath.

"So you do still feel it?" he asked.

"You bastard! Jesus, Mother, Mary and Joseph." Rosalie crossed herself. "You really are out of this world, you came from hell to make everyone's life a misery."

"Look, how serious is this new guy?"

"What?" For a second Rosalie was confused, and then she remembered the sinner/saviour conversation.

"Serious."

"What does he look like?"

"Why? Want to swap tips?"

"No."

"Then what?"

"I just want to see if you really are moving on or just got a new guy to annoy me."

"How would tell that from looks?"

Nothing ventured, nothing gained

"Well, if you got a temporary guy to annoy me, then he wouldn't be that good looking because you wouldn't be that serious. However, if he is serious, he'd be good looking because you'd be planning a future with him." Jack smiled. "Even babies and you don't want ugly babies."

"You are just....." Rosalie didn't finish her sentence because she saw a tall figure coming towards her, with black hair, a lot of muscle bulging through his t-shirt and jeans, his funny brown eyes glistening and laughing and his walk, all confidence and sexuality. Then Rosalie snapped out of her ogling fest and took the situation in. Damn! Jack would assume Matt was the new man, but obviously Matt wasn't the new man. Not yet, anyway. She ran towards Matthew, who couldn't have disguised his surprise if he'd tried and threw her arms around his neck. He seemed to hesitate about putting his arms around her back, but when he did and got a tight grip, Rosalie's stomach let out a bout of little flip-flops and tingles shot around her body.

"Just go along with it, please," she whispered into his ear, then pulled back from Matthew and looked into his brown eyes. Just like her own, she thought.

She turned to Jack and put her arm around Matthew's waist. He copied her movement, but she felt his body tense. God, she must be repulsive to cuddle after a day of sweating, she thought.

"Jack Blindle, meet Matthew..." She faltered. "Maybrew," she said, in a slight questioning tone looking at him. He just smiled at her.

"Hi," he said to Jack.

"How are you today?" Jack asked back.

"Not bad. Yourself?"

"I'm very well."

"So, Lee, you didn't tell me about this dark horse."

Matthew looked at Rosalie and she beamed at him. "Well, we wanted it to be a secret, until we knew we were serious about each other."

Matthew's eyebrows shot up, clearly getting more than he bargained for.

Rosalie shifted against his body so they would get closer, and despite the fact that this was a situation she hated, being next to Matthew's body wasn't a bad thing at all. In fact she rather liked it.

Matthew drew her closer to him, telling himself that it was for the show he and Rosalie were putting up for this guy, but if he was honest with himself, he just wanted to get closer. When she'd flung herself at him, his breath had been knocked out of his lungs as her breasts had flattened against him, her wonderful scent engulfing all his senses, making all his pulse points flare and quicken their pace.

"Yes," Matthew said, clearing his voice and pushing his thoughts to one side. "It's been at least five months now," he added, then realised he'd said the wrong thing by the panic in Rosalie's eyes.

Jack looked uncomfortable. "So, you guys have been seeing each other before I got married?" He looked at Rosalie, who nodded.

He then looked at Matthew. "Sorry, I just calculate

Nothing ventured, nothing gained

things to my wedding these days; you know how much stress they cause."

"Well, we're hoping to," Rosalie said.

"Sure you are," Jack answered, looking intently at Rosalie, who was looking at Matthew and him back at her. She saw the slight glint of mischief in his eyes and knew he was going to kiss her. He dropped his head slowly and brought his lips to hers in a light kiss. If Rosalie wasn't aware of her heartbeat racing, she would have sworn it hadn't happened. They both looked back at Jack.

"Well, I gotta go. See you soon, Lee. Oh, and let's go through the bible and see what sins we've committed." He stared at her for a second, then nodded at Matthew and walked away.

Both Rosalie and Matthew stood staring after Jack's retreating back, and then reluctantly separated.

"What was that all about?" Matthew asked.

"Sorry. Would you be willing to take the answer it was an impulse of mine?"

"What's the real answer?"

"Too long and boring."

He was silent as he took her appearance in. God, she was beautiful, he thought. Those brown eyes, which had haunted him so many times in his sleep and dreams, were staring at him, amused and grateful.

"Fine. Anyway, thank you for your impulse, it was nice."

"You are very welcome."

"Shall I act on my other impulses or just be a gentleman?" he asked with a grin. The difference,

Rosalie thought, was that Matthew could be arrogant, with a massive ego, but could still be serious at the same time. He could make suggestions and flirt with her, but not in a perverted way, he said it in a funny way as if for his amusement as well as her own. He's not afraid to make a prat of himself, she thought, and probably has never been embarrassed. Well, let's see if I'm capable of making the man blush.

"You see this cross?" She held up a small silver cross from around her neck. Matthew nodded.

"I live by this symbol."

"How so?" he asked, pursing his lips.

"I'm Catholic. I follow the religion like a chick follows…the mother hen." Rosalie cringed at her words.

"Strange analogy."

"Well, I never said I was a poet."

"OK then, please tell me what the Catholic religion tells you to do."

"I don't believe in abortion," she stated, looking into his eyes for disapproval. She didn't find any.

"OK."

"I don't believe in euthanasia, it is murder."

"Fine," he nodded.

"I don't condone suicide. Only God gave life, only he can take it away."

"I agree."

Rosalie drew a blank. She had never been good at religion at school. She hesitated as she noted that Matthew didn't look that scared or put off by her tactic of making him seem embarrassed. In fact he seemed intrigued. She then decided to hit

Nothing ventured, nothing gained

him with the cruncher.
"I don't believe in sex before marriage," she said with a smile.
Matthew was stumped for a second. Then he noted the briefest flicker of amusement in Rosalie's eyes and knew he'd been had. Knew she was doing it on purpose.
"I respect that," he replied.
She fumed. "I mean I don't believe in sex at all."
"Yeah, I understand, I mean a woman has to look out for herself these days."
"I would probably have artificial insemination to have children. Sex is a sin."
"I thought artificial insemination was against the Catholic religion."
She looked confused at him.
"I guess I neglected to tell you the fact that I'm from Ireland and I come from a Catholic family."
"Bollocks."
He watched her eyes look down at the floor, then saw her lips twitch upward. He loved the way her face betrayed her true feelings and that she was capable of taking a joke that had been made at her expense, even if she was the one who started it.
"So, what are you doing here?" she asked. He stared down at her. Good question, he thought, what am I doing here? Sure, originally it was to make a deal that would hopefully benefit both of them, but as soon as he saw her running towards him with an anxious smile on her face, all thinking had ceased. He watched her brown eyes looking back at him and decided that Rosalie was a

private woman, but also had a flamboyant personality which shone through the darkest days.
"Well, I came to offer you something."
"Jesus, if you say something to do with the reproductive system…"
"No!" Matthew exclaimed, laughing. "I was going to offer you a proposition."
"Proposition?"
"Yeah."
"Oh." They were both silent.
"Let's go to dinner and I'll discuss it with you then."
"So, it's like a business dinner?" she asked, squinting her eyes against the sun, making it hard to tell Matthew's expression.
"Yeah. A business dinner."
"OK. Where?"
"Well, I'll pick you up."
"At my house?" Rosalie's voice suddenly got higher.
"Is that a problem?"
"No. it's just…well, it's in a bit of a state and my brother will be there as well as Sucker."
"Sucker?"
"My new dog. Well, a loan dog. He's over there." Rosalie pointed to where Sucker was laying in the sun, tongue hanging out of his mouth and looking very content.
"He looks…very active," Matthew said with a grin.
"Well…he's kind of overweight, but gorgeous on the inside."
"Of course."
"'Cos it's what's on the inside that matters."
"Indeed it is."

Nothing ventured, nothing gained

They looked at each other.
"Well, I live at Harpsden, in a cottage. I'll wait on the main road. But if I'm not there, my cottage is the white one with a hell of a lot of flowers."
"Do you like gardening?"
"God no! Gwen does it."
"Gwen?"
"Surrogate mother," Rosalie answered with a nod. Matthew nodded too, as if it all made perfect sense.
"See you then," he said.
"Sure," she answered, with a grin.
He began to walk away when she called out his name.
"Sorry about earlier… with Jack. He's…kind of arrogant. Like you," she added with a grin.
Matthew nodded and grinned too. "No problem." He turned to walk away. "By the way, my surname is Mason."

Chapter six

Gwen looked around the crowded room and saw the woman sitting by the window. The social club, purely for pensioners, was used for a good gossip and a cup of Earl Grey. Gwen hated it, as she still thought of herself as rather young, but if she ever needed information on someone, this was the place to go. She cared for Rosalie and Neus just like she would if she had ever had children of her own. But her husband hadn't wanted any, which now she thought of a blessing in disguise, as she had found out about his affairs with half the village of Harpsden all those years ago.
Gwen proceeded towards the woman and took in her profile. She was pensive, and not at all what she had expected. She looked frail yet sharp. She seemed in her own world, but Gwen could see her eyes taking everyone and everything in. I'm doing this for Rose, she told herself as she tapped the woman on the shoulder. After all, Gwen had seen the heartache and pain Rosalie had been through. Jack, her parents, and she always remembered the lonely nights when Rosalie would come over to her cottage because Neus was away. Rosalie had dedicated most of her teenage and adult life to Neus, looking after him, making sure he was safe. Gwen knew that their bond was stronger than anything, probably by Rosalie looking out for him when they were younger while travelling with their parents. When they had both moved to the cottage, Gwen couldn't help but notice that they seemed in need of help. That's when she had

Nothing ventured, nothing gained

made her infamous apple crumble and took it over to them. She would never forget their expression when they'd smelt and tasted a home-cooked pudding. Perhaps they had saved each other from loneliness, as Gwen's husband had left a short time after she had discovered all his infidelities, and when Neus was away or Rosalie left for a horse event, Gwen was always with the other one. But she was saddened when she felt the full brunt of being seventy and questioned her own mortality. She had never allowed herself to think about death, she had decided it was a depressing matter and one she would happily put off, which is why she never made a will and lived each day to the fullest. However, it was the death of her friend Elizabeth which had jolted her back to reality with a landing that had shaken her bones. Or maybe it was the bruises that had suddenly appeared, or perhaps the aching muscles. Gwen didn't know when or what had made her start feeling old, but she did know that she didn't like it and would try everything in her power to stop it happening. Which, she told herself now as she sat down facing this woman, she would do after she had made Rosalie and Neus happy. Gwen had came to the conclusion that the best way to enjoy old age (and not get so many wrinkles) was make sure that one's loved ones were happy and enjoying life. And Rosalie and Neus were her only loved ones. Therefore, thought Gwen, this is how she can make them both happy.

"Hello, I'm Gwen Baxter," she said, extending her hand to be shaken. The woman raised her eyebrows, but shook her hand anyway.

"I think we can help each other," Gwen said, sitting down and crossing her legs. The woman copied the same position and regarded her with a curious expression.

"How so?" the woman asked.

"Well…first of all, it is customary for you to give your name and then we talk," Gwen said, with a smile.

"Well, I presume you already know my name, otherwise why would you be here?" the woman asked.

"It is courtesy."

"Please, we are in a room full of busy gossip queens, who to be quite frank do not have any gossip worth knowing." The woman irritably smoothed her skirt down and frowned her eyebrows at Gwen. "If you are here to tell me something about my son, then I would rather you didn't. Gossip is precisely that – gossip. Not truth." The woman uncrossed her legs and made to get up just as Gwen put her hand on her arm.

"You want your son to be happy; I want my surrogate daughter to be happy. We can help each other and make the kids happy." Gwen smiled and the woman sat down again.

"Surrogate daughter?"

"She is the daughter I never had."

The woman looked at Gwen, then around them. She sat thoughtfully for a few minutes, and in this time Gwen was praying that she would agree to help; otherwise she didn't know how to make Rosalie happy. Finally, the woman looked up and

Nothing ventured, nothing gained

smiled.
"I'm Beth Mason."

"Damn!.... AHHH!"
Neus ran upstairs after hearing the massive thud vibrate throughout the cottage.
"Lee?" he shouted as he raced to her bedroom. He was downstairs making his dinner when he heard the massive thud. It was always a nightmare Neus had when he was little. Someone breaking into his bedroom through the window, and everyone else downstairs laughing at the television, while this murderer slit his throat and threw him on the floor. The massive thud of the dead body always used to wake him up in a cold sweat. "Lee?" he shouted again as he rounded the corner to her bedroom and without knocking, raced into it and looked around for her body. Seeing Rosalie lying on the floor, groaning, as a pile of clothes and a basket were spread over her body, hadn't been what he'd expected. There was no blood, no man with a knife and no dead body; instead, there was a woman buried alive by the Persil scent of clean clothes. Neus tried hard not to laugh. Underneath the pile of clothes, Rosalie sighed and groaned again. It was just her luck that as she was looking for her favourite baby blue shirt, the whole shelf of clothes fell on her. And as she was running late, she was sure God was working against her. But what annoyed Rosalie the most was that Neus was laughing at her, and he wasn't making any attempt to help her up.
"Well, are you going to help me or just keep

laughing?" she snapped, her voice muffled by a sock in her mouth. Neus reached for her hand and pulled her up, sending various items of clothing through the air and landing on the furniture.

"How, um, did you do this?" Neus asked, picking a pair of knickers from her shoulder.

"I was reaching for that jumper," she said, pointing to the top shelf. Neus sighed and easily lifted his hand and gave the jumper to Rosalie.

"You make it look easy," she grumbled as she ran her hands over the creases. "Shit, look at this!" she exclaimed, thrusting the shirt in his face.

"What do you want me to do about it?" he asked, backing towards the door as each word went by.

"Oi! Come back here and iron this!"

"No, I'm making food," he objected. Rosalie took a deep breath to steady her nerves and temper.

"You have to because Matthew is picking me up in…" She looked at her watch. "Oh shit, ten minutes and I haven't even showered to get rid of horse smells."

"Yeah, you do smell pretty bad," Neus said as Rosalie swept past him to start the shower.

"Yeah, I sort of fell into the muck heap and tripped over the garlic powder."

"How do you do this to yourself?" he asked, picking a sock off her leg.

"Beats me. If I knew, I wouldn't bloody do it," she said as she shut the door in his face and he heard her opening the shower door.

Neus returned to the kitchen and found the iron. He thought about Rosalie and Matthew. He hadn't really thought of his sister ever having a serious

Nothing ventured, nothing gained

boyfriend, but it seemed to Neus that Matthew sounded serious, even though Rosalie had argued he didn't mean anything. But when a person denies that they like someone, Neus thought as he began to iron the shirt, it was always serious.

Upstairs, Rosalie was having a massive problem blow drying her hair. It wouldn't do anything she asked it to. Dear God, she thought, not even the strongest gel could help her now. She looked in the mirror and sighed. Why couldn't she have time to get ready for dates like every other woman? She thought how great it would be to have time to put on a face mask, paint her nails, apply her make-up several times before she got it perfect, and get her hair done properly. Instead, she now had five minutes to get dressed, apply make-up, and somehow get her hair into a half-decent state. All Rosalie hoped was that Matthew wasn't the punctual type, because if he actually got here in five minutes, he would be waiting for a while. Dear God, she thought, he'd be talking to Neus. This last thought spurred her into action. She decided to leave her hair to its own devices and she turned to her make-up. A quick dab of eye shadow, a thin line of eyeliner, a stroke of blusher, and then a few swipes of mascara. There, she thought, looking at her reflection, all done. Rosalie peered closer into the mirror and noticed she hadn't done her bottom lashes. She pulled the mascara out and gently swiped them with the wand.
"Lee!" shouted Neus up the stairs, causing Rosalie

to jump and poke herself in the eye with the mascara wand. "Fuck!" she said as she wiped her eyes clean of pain. Then it occurred to her that she was smudging the rest of her make-up and she quickly pulled her arm away. Losing her balance, she fell head first onto the floor, this time without the soft clothes as a cushion.

Neus opened the door to Matthew and let him pass, then turned around and took in his profile. Neus noticed his black hair and brown eyes. Good combination, he thought, Lee always suited men with dark hair and dark eyes. Although he couldn't recall her ever dating someone who had the same colour eyes as hers.
"I'm her brother, Neus."
"Yeah, she mentioned you." He offered his hand. "Good to meet you."
Neus and Matthew shook hands.
"She mentioned you as well," Neus said.
"She did?" Matthew asked, liking that she had mentioned him, but afraid of how she mentioned him.
"Yeah." They were both silent.
"Lee!" Neus shouted. He looked at Matthew and smiled. "Ever since we were little children, I have always had to wait for her. Wait here, I'll go and get her." He bounded up the stairs. Rosalie was frantically washing off all her make-up when Neus knocked on the door.
"Lee, he's here."
"Shit!" she hissed.
"Can I come in?"

Nothing ventured, nothing gained

"No, I look a fucking state. Damn mascara wand," she muttered, looking at the discarded mascara laying on the floor where she had thrown it in a temper.
"He's waiting, and maybe it's best not to leave him waiting long?" Neus suggested.

Rosalie stared at herself in the mirror. She looked red and blotchy, partly from rubbing her face so hard and from crying. She sometimes envied all those other girls who always looked squeaky clean and presented themselves like a proper lady. And here she was, clothes creased, face red and spirits down. She took one last look in the mirror and began to smile. Since she was little and had felt rejected by her parents, she had always put on her brave face. She stuck her chin out, straightened her shoulders and smiled. She smiled at whoever looked at her; she'd smile at grumpy traffic wardens, at tramps on the streets and even at rude road rage drivers. It was her brave face that she used quite often. So tonight, she would use it again.

Matthew's face was a picture when he saw Rosalie. She couldn't help notice that the picture didn't display annoyance or disgust, purely amusement and affection. That's scary, she thought as she got her coat. Matthew held her coat open for her to step into and smelled her scent of shampoo. He briefly closed his eyes at the scent, then snapped them open again, but not before Neus saw his reaction. It was funny, Neus thought, how transparent an emotion can make you.

"Thank you," Rosalie said as she opened the door. "Now, Neus, eat properly and look after Sucker."

"Yeah, sure. You crazy kids have fun," he said as he shut the door and raced upstairs to look out of the window.

Without realising they were being watched, Rosalie and Matthew got into his car. He pulled away from the cottage and drove along Harpsden Lane.

"Your brother is nice," Matthew said.

"He is. We are quite close."

"I noticed."

"You did, did you?" she asked, turning to face him, smiling.

He glanced at her. "Yeah. He seems…. protective."

Rosalie snorted. "I can't imagine what he was protecting me from."

"Maybe you don't want to find out," Matthew answered.

"Hmmm. Well, as long as you keep your mind on this…proposition of yours, I assured Neus I would be safe."

"Where else would my mind wander?" he asked as he turned onto the Reading Road.

"You tell me."

He laughed. "I don't think we're capable of having a serious conversation."

"We haven't tried."

"Suppose not."

They were silent for a minute or two. "Where are

Nothing ventured, nothing gained

we going?"
"Villa Marina."
"The Italian place?" Rosalie asked excitedly.
"Yeah," Matthew answered, amused at her reaction. "Have you been there before?"
"Once with..." Rosalie stopped as the word "Jack" was about to be spoken aloud. She didn't want to think about Jack or about how Matthew had acted as her boyfriend, or that light kiss they had shared. "Once with a friend," she said instead. He nodded, allowing that excuse to be used.
"Well, we're going there tonight."
"Yey."
"Yey?"
"What?" she asked, narrowing her eyebrows.
"Nothing. Just you."
"Me?"
Matthew just smiled as she looked at him waiting an explanation.
"Forget it. You are not getting one."
The rest of the drive was spent in silence.

They sat opposite each other, eyes firmly attached to their menus, deciding what to have. Rosalie couldn't help the way her stomach was fluttering or the tingles that had started from when Matthew's hand had grazed her arm when he took her coat off. Nor could she help the permanent goose bumps that hadn't gone from her skin since leaving the cottage. She stole a quick glance at him and saw he was concentrating, almost as hard as she was, on the choices of food. If Rosalie were honest, she hadn't even begun to study the menu; she'd been too busy making sure Matthew didn't see her looking at him. Of course, she knew the way she looked at him betrayed her feelings that she wasn't yet ready to deal with, and she also realised that if he discovered how she felt, Matthew would have the upper hand, and God forbid a man to have the advantage!

She looked at the menu and prayed her eyes would take in the words.

OK, she told herself, Steak loin, Duck….

Matthew's brown eyed lifted slightly, so he could see Rosalie's face over the top of his menu. Perhaps he should have felt embarrassed about her choice of clothes in a restaurant like this, he mused, like his father had been on so many occasions before. But he tried to find fault with her appearance, anything that would show him that what he was feeling was purely a testosterone attack and nothing more. And by finding fault with her, he would begin to dislike her, and then ultimately they wouldn't meet again. Somehow, that plan didn't seem like it would work. She wasn't an obvious beauty, Matthew thought as he took a sip of wine, nothing like all the models he had dated. But, he reminded himself, all those models had going for them were their looks.

Rosalie's mid-length brown hair hung loosely around her shoulders. It wasn't straightened to perfection nor curled so tightly it looked as if it would pop. It simply hung there, untamed, taking on a life of its own. That was good, he thought, that means she wouldn't worry about how her hair looked when he took her to his bed. Which he

Nothing ventured, nothing gained

planned to do soon. Her brown eyes allowed him to guess that she was feeling the same desire and attraction, which contributed to the awkwardness between them. He wanted to say something, even something arrogant, anything to get the conversation rolling, but he suddenly felt nervous. Him! Matthew Mason, top PR agent, nervous! If his friends saw him now, they would never believe it. But being with Rosalie somehow made it OK to be nervous. It reminded him that he was only human after all, and humans aren't immune to feeling nervous. Even if you're in a job where nervousness causes a problem. She looked up and caught him staring.

Brown eyes met brown eyes and neither person made any sign of breaking the stare.

Rosalie had felt his gaze on her only moments before, like burning a hole into her skin. A nice hole, she reminded herself, she just hadn't liked being studied. Attention was something she didn't feel comfortable with. Rosalie had always been the girl in the school production who did the make-up or lighting back stage. As a woman, she had always been the one to tag along and watch the action of her friends instead of being the one who caused it. Although her friends always got this fact wrong. They always assumed Rosalie was the woman with all the flair, who danced in the middle of the crowd and who started talking to strangers. She had once done those things in the past, but preferred to stay in the background. This is why now she wasn't so keen on Matthew staring at her face. Looking deeply into her eyes, as if searching for something. She stared back into his dark eyes. Was it just her, or did their eyes seem to melt into each other? She thought she could detect a hint of affection, desire in spades and amusement. Definitely amusement. Damn him for laughing at me, she thought, although she didn't break the stare. He was the first one to look away, and Rosalie would have felt a small triumph if he hadn't moved his gaze onto her lips. She felt them tremble under his ever watchful gaze, and felt a rush of desire flare within her body, hitting every pulse point as it travelled to her head to make her feel dizzy. Rosalie had heard her friends say they went dizzy with desire, but had never really thought it true. Until now, with Matthew still looking at her red lips, her head spun and spun as if on the teacup ride at Thorpe Park.

"Would you quit staring?" she snapped, putting a hand to her temple and applying pressure. She looked at his smiling face and knew he was being his usual smug self.

"I can't help it," he said.

"Yeah, sure."

The waiter came up and took their orders, then scuttled off towards the kitchens.

Rosalie leant forward and rested her elbows on the table.

"I feel under-dressed," she said, looking around her at all the other diners.

"You look beautiful," he said. "Now, this proposition."

Rosalie shook her head as if to clear it. He had given her a compliment, but then just as quickly as

Nothing ventured, nothing gained

it had come, he had moved onto another subject.
"Right." She cleared her throat. "This proposition. Tell me."
"OK." He leant back in his chair and looked at her face lit by the small candle. "Basically, the night we met, Kevin, my mate." He snorted. "Well, ex-mate, was telling me the trouble he was in."
Rosalie raised her eyebrows, intrigued.
"He got this girl, Robin Lotte, pregnant. I don't know if you've heard of her…"
"Robin Lotte?" Rosalie asked. "The heiress to Kurt Lotte's businesses and estates?"
Matthew nodded.
"Jeez…she's got a lot to inherit."
"Yes, she has, but…"
"Hold, on…she's engaged to Count Vicro, the count of…um…"
"Yes, I know," Matthew said nodding. "Which means getting pregnant by a low-life like Kevin wasn't a very good idea."
"Anyway, I saw Kevin, why did she sleep with him?" Rosalie asked to try to lighten the mood.
Matthew laughed. "God knows. But she doesn't want to marry this guy. She wants to have the baby and she's making Kevin help out."
"Too right."
He ignored Rosalie's comment. "But Kevin had nowhere to put her. I mean, he has nothing to give her. So he called on me for help." Matthew took a sip of wine again and ran a hand down his face. "Basically, I don't have anywhere for her to stay. I need somewhere secretive because if people find out she's staying with me, gossip will get out and

the next thing you know, I'd be marrying her." He looked horrified by the idea and Rosalie had to admit she wasn't too thrilled by it either.

"So, this is where you come in." he said with a grin.

"Hold on. How come you don't want people knowing? I mean, who really cares about what you're doing?"

"I'm a PR agent," he said, his ego hating the fact that she didn't know what he did and his mind loving the fact that she didn't read all the gossip columns, otherwise she would have heard of him.

"Cool. Have you represented anyone I know?"

He laughed, and then nodded. "Sure. Kate Gayle, Chip McGill, Boop Walker." He mentioned a few

Rosalie's mouth was practically open and laying on the table. "That's amazing. How come I've never heard of you?"

"Well... I take it you don't read *Clarke Times* or *Hello!* Or even *OK!*"

"I glance at them sometimes. But just at the pictures."

"Well, if you read them, you'd hear about how great I am, how my magic brain has done it again. And you would read about the models I've dated."

"Jesus, can your ego get any bigger?"

"I'm sure it can. And it just did."

"What?"

"Well, you looked impressed when I mentioned those stars, so now I've got a massive ego." He leant back in his chair and crossed his legs, smiling an ear-splitting grin. That grin made Rosalie want to punch it off his face. So arrogant,

Nothing ventured, nothing gained

she thought, but she couldn't ignore the tingling feeling she felt whenever he grinned at her, arrogant or otherwise. He leant forward so their faces were only inches apart and dropped his voice, which to Rosalie's ears sounded arrogant and sexy as hell.
"Or maybe I just have a massive hard-on?"
Rosalie's mouth dropped open and her breath caught in her throat. "You're despicable," she hissed, clearing her throat and looking around to make sure no one had heard him. Matthew adjusted his legs so that their knees touched. A massive ping erupted throughout Rosalie's body, making her jump and frown at him.
"You have no scruples, do you? You just do as you please." Rosalie moved her knees away and crossed her legs. "Well, you're about to learn that you can't use me as you please."
"I wouldn't use you as I please, I'd make sure you were well compensated for the position you would put yourself in."
Rosalie's mouth once again flew open in disbelief. Was he actually offering her money for sex? The God damn nerve!
"My position?"
"Yes. I realise that it would be difficult to put yourself in that position, but I'd make sure you were looked after." He smiled. "I'm sure it's not the first time anyway."
Rosalie frowned her eyebrows and narrowed her eyes. Not the first time she'd had sex? He has a nerve to insinuate I'm a slapper, she thought. Rosalie felt a sweep of anger come over her and

decided she wasn't going to take this. "I appreciate the 'position' you would like me to take, but I can assure you that I do not in any way accept money for sex, and the fact that you would actually fucking offer it in the first place is an insult to me. Yes, I've had sex before, quite a few times, with a few people, and yes, I am very good." She rushed on as Matthew made to interrupt. "Not that you would ever find that fact out for yourself. And no, I'm afraid to disappoint you, I haven't been offered money before and even if I had I would have the same reply as now. Even if it was through a time when I needed money." She looked at him. "I'm not a whore and I thought you weren't a seedy git, but now you've offered me that 'position' I have changed my mind and think you're a fucking, arrogant, jumped-up little shit."

She sat back in her chair and uncrossed her legs so their knees touched again. She ignored the tingling, and started feeling angry with herself that she could still find him attractive. Then she noticed the surprise and shock on his face. A waiter stood close by, wearing the same expression, then Rosalie looked around and noticed that everyone was looking at their table, all wearing that I-can't-believe-it expression. A blush crept up her face and she suddenly had the horrible thought that maybe she was wrong at what Matthew had been talking about. She had let herself be taken away by her anger and hadn't even realised that she had been shouting. Rosalie opened her mouth to say something, then closed it as she had no idea what to say. Some murmurings had risen within

Nothing ventured, nothing gained

the restaurant and the waiter had gone, but the majority were still staring at her, including Matthew. She looked at him and looked into those eyes, silently laughing at her expense. Suddenly she didn't want to be in this place any more and she didn't want those brown eyes looking at her. She grabbed her coat and handbag and ran for the exit. She was saddened not to hear Matthew's voice call after her.

Chapter seven

"You're an idiot, Lee," Neus said, making her a cup of tea and passing it to her.
"I know. Last night, was just….I made a prat of myself."
He laughed. "Ah well, we all do it."
"Yeah, but why does it have to happen to me?" Rosalie pouted into her cup.
"Oh dear, is this a self-pity routine?"
Rosalie looked sharply up at Neus. "Course it bloody is. Why wouldn't it be? I think I'm entitled to it."
"Oh dear," Neus said as he rinsed out his mug and set it by the sink.
"Don't sound like that."
"Why?"
"He sounds like that," Rosalie answered, pouting again.
"He is, I take it, Matthew?"
"Course."
"Why did I sound like him?"
"Arrogant and an arsehole," she said as she walked out of the kitchen.
"Sympathy for the Devil" vibrated through Rosalie's eardrums as she mucked out Merlin's stable. She thought the song fitting for her I-hate-Matthew day.
Of course, Rosalie had tired to ignore the feeling of such emptiness in her stomach and concentrate on eating until it felt full. She knew she didn't hate Matthew, in fact she liked him, a lot, but it was easier to pretend she didn't care and to hate him.

Nothing ventured, nothing gained

But she couldn't ignore the fact that he hadn't come after her, or even made sure she got home safely. Rosalie knew it was pointless, because even if he had come out after her, she would have just told him to go away; but still, he could have offered.

There was a tap on her shoulder and for a fleeting moment Rosalie could feel the hope that it would be Matthew sprang to life, but when she turned and saw Jack, that hope left her body and the miserable gloom set in again.

"Original Prankster" by the Offspring started playing in Rosalie's ears as she looked at Jack and didn't disguise her annoyance in her sigh. She pulled one earphone out of her ear and left the other one in.

"Yeah?" she asked.

"Just wondering if you still like being a saviour."

Rosalie tried to recall the conversation they'd had, then laughed.

"Jeez, are you still going on about that?"

Jack looked slightly put out at her response but recovered quickly as he moved in towards her and place a hand on her hip.

She looked down at the hand and then back at him. "You really have a massive idiotic nerve."

Jack grinned that self-assured grin, which made her think of Matthew; only Matthew's always caused goose bumps. Jack's grin did nothing for her.

Her eyes fixed on an object behind and smiled at Jack.

"In fact, your nerve is right on target. Come on

then, let's hop into the bush." She pulled his hand around her waist and brought him closer. Jack's grin disappeared but his breathing slowed.

"Maybe we could invite your wife for a threesome?" Rosalie asked as she let him go and turned him around to see his wife coming up the yard. She felt Jack's spine stiffen and saw sweat break out on his upper lip.

"Cigarettes and Alcohol" came on as Rosalie pushed him forward towards his wife. Jack went obediently, smiling sheepishly and pulling Mary in for a kiss. Rosalie turned her back and carried on with her mucking out.

"Tili really is a nice girl," Beth said as she placed her teacup on the table. Gwen nodded, knowing she was and that she would be perfect for Neus.

"She just…..needs to blossom. And stop pining for my Matthew," Beth said with a knowing nod. Gwen agreed, then smiled.

"I hope Matthew hasn't gone off my Rose since that dinner a couple of days ago," Gwen said, remembering how Rosalie had come over to her house last night and poured her heart out. Neus had left for another modelling job and Rosalie needed someone to talk to. Gwen had been more than happy to listen, as now she could find out more information and that would bring her and Beth one step closer to bringing them together.

Beth shook her head. "If anything, he just seems happier. He keeps smiling and offering to help for any matter I have."

"But he was like that before," Gwen pointed out,

Nothing ventured, nothing gained

remembering how she and Beth had both praised Rosalie and Matthew when describing them.
"Yes, he was. But since that dinner, it feels as if he's floating on air. That girl of yours definitely has something about her."
"She does."
"And what about Rose? Has she gone of my Matthew?"
"Quite the opposite, Beth. She tells herself and me that she hates him, but of course she doesn't. It is just easier for her to deal with rejection that way."
"He hasn't rejected her!" Beth objected.
"No, but she thinks he has. After all, it's been two days since the dinner."
"Yes, well. I'm quite sure that Matthew is just thinking of how to approach her, how to court her properly," Beth said wistfully, thinking of how her husband had courted her.
"You see, the thing is, Rose is someone with confidence, but she does still need reassurance. So if Matthew were to, let's say, go and see her and assure her he still likes her, then Rose will be so very happy."
Beth pondered this idea. "I do understand, Gwen, but Matthew doesn't think I know anything about Rose and if I were to interrupt…"
"Yes, I am in the same position with Rose. But if you were to nudge him…I don't know, to go up to the Acorn stables or take you to Pitter Patter…"
"He wouldn't go up there as he knows Rose will be there," Beth pointed out. Both women sat in silence.
"My mother used to say that if God wants it and

love is strong enough, it will happen on its own," Gwen said, unsure if they should get involved.
"My father told me that if you want something, you have to go out and get it," Beth responded.
They both thought their own thoughts for a while.
"We'll leave it for two days and if nothing happens, then we'll intervene," Gwen said.
"Good compromise," Beth responded, picking up her tea again.

Matthew got out of his car and searched for the familiar body. He couldn't see her anywhere and wondered where he should start. Acorn stables was an easy enough place to find, as it was near his house in Hambledon, but searching for Rosalie proved to be a more difficult task. He hadn't seen her in three days and it surprised and irritated him that he missed her so much. When they went out, he was sure he was getting in too deep, that he was beginning to feel things about her that he hadn't felt before. Then when she'd shouted at him for offering money for sex, he knew he was hooked. The way her brown eyes flashed when she was angry, the way her chest heaved up and down with her anger and her hair moving around as she had shouted at him....the scene had stayed in his mind ever since. He tried hard not to think about what her lips had looked like when she was saying the words, but that image still haunted him. Every time he thought of it, a grin spread across his face and his mind went dizzy on lust and genuine affection for her. She was definitely one of kind, he had decided. But he

Nothing ventured, nothing gained

needed an answer from her about the proposition of Robin staying at her house. Even though he hadn't actually got as far as mentioning it, he was sure she had got the gist of what he was offering.
"Look, just piss off and leave me alone!" he heard a woman's voice say. He was certain it was Rosalie. He walked around the corner to where he thought it had come from and saw a door closed, but the window was open.
"Listen, you and me, we're meant to be. We're soul mates," said a male voice.
Matthew stopped dead and listened carefully.
"My God! You men are just like each other!" she exclaimed. "Always so sure of yourself and so full of shit."
Matthew winced at the venom in her voice. Obviously she had come to that conclusion with a little help from him.
"We're not, baby, come on, you're too good for that Matthew."
Matthew frowned his eyebrows. He leant closer when he couldn't hear anything.
"Yes," she said in a quiet voice. "Yes, I am too good for him. But you know what? I'm too fucking good for you as well!"
Matthew instantly ducked when he heard a crash. It took him a few seconds to realise she probably had thrown something at the man in the room.
"For Christ sake! Calm down!" he heard the man shout.
"Piss off!"
"Are you fucking crazy?"
"Yes, I'm crazy! I'm so crazy that I should be

locked up, so why don't you piss off, otherwise I'll get a hell of a lot crazier!"

A man ran past Matthew with such speed that he had to blink a few times before he realised that the man had gone. Matthew walked around the corner and saw Rosalie leaning against the counter, arms outstretched in front of her, breathing heavily. He wasn't sure if she was crying and he didn't want to disturb her, but he found he couldn't walk away. He noticed that her hair was plastered to her neck with sweat. She must have been working hard, he thought. Her shorts complimented her long legs, which Matthew had dreamt about since he met her, although he didn't like to admit it to himself. Her strappy top clung to her body and enhanced her figure. It was only May, yet the sun was out and shining bright and temperatures were warm. Matthew thought about using the weather as an excuse for why he felt so hot, but deep down he knew better. He looked at Rosalie and decided he'd come back tomorrow or drop by the cottage tomorrow evening.

Gwen allowed the waiter to take off her coat as she led Rosalie to their table, which she had specifically requested. The Green Olive, in Henley, was surprising in a pleasant way. Gwen had never been there herself before, and was sure Rosalie didn't come here often either. She took her seat and thanked the waiter as he handed her the menu. She glanced at Rosalie and felt guilt and pleasure at taking her out to dinner. Rosalie

Nothing ventured, nothing gained

hadn't made much of an effort to get dressed up, and if Gwen were to mention it, Rosalie would have become suspicious. So, Gwen had kept her comments to herself and only hoped things would go according to how she and Beth had planned.
Rosalie looked down at the menu and let out a sigh. It had been one week since that disastrous dinner with Matthew and ever since then she'd been feeling down. On the many occasions when she tortured herself by re-playing the dinner over in her head, she was now sure Matthew hadn't been offering money for sex; in fact, Rosalie was now embarrassed and baffled at how she had came to that conclusion.
"This is nice, isn't it?" Gwen asked, laying her menu down and looking at Rosalie.
"Yes."
"When does Neus get back?"
"Wednesday, I think," Rosalie answered.
"So, what are you going to have?"
"Um, probably the steak or something."
"Good. Some nice red meat will be good for you."
"Good for me?"
"Yes."
Rosalie looked at Gwen and smiled. She always acted as the mother hen, knowing what was best.
"Well, I guess you're right. Damn it," she said as her bracelet fell onto the floor.
"Oh, does it always come off?"
"Yeah," Rosalie answered, pushing her chair back and looking for it. "I got it from a crappy Spanish market when I went with Neus last year. Ah!" she said when she spotted it. If Rosalie had been

sitting on her chair she would have seen Matthew and Beth Mason walk into the restaurant. She would also have seen the conspicuous wink shared between Beth and Gwen.

"Here it is!" Rosalie announced proudly as she sat back on her chair and showed the bracelet to Gwen. She inspected the bracelet with false delight; she was too concerned whether or not Rosalie would notice Matthew sitting a few tables down. She and Beth had planned it so that they both sat in the curve of the restaurant, with a good view of the tables around them. Gwen had also pointed out that she and Beth would need to be back to back, so Matthew had to sit opposite Beth, each with a good view of the other.

Then when Matthew sat down and Rosalie saw him, they assumed they would smile and sit together, and then Beth and Gwen would go and have a cup of tea. Rosalie dropping her bracelet was pure luck. Beth and Gwen had given it three days, as they agreed, but nothing had happened. They had then started planning the dinner idea, then decided to do it on the exact same day Rosalie and Matthew had had dinner last week.

"Yes Rose, it is a very fine piece of jewellery," Gwen commented, her eyes darting from side to side, trying to see Matthew or Beth; but then of course, she realised, that would be easier if she wasn't sitting back to back to Beth.

"Gwen, it isn't. It was two euros, for Christ's sake and it wasn't even worth the…" Rosalie stopped talking and Gwen saw her eyes widen in shock and surprise. Bingo! Gwen thought, she's spotted

Nothing ventured, nothing gained

him. Rosalie cleared her throat nosily and quickly looked down to her bracelet.
"What's wrong, dear?" Gwen asked.
Rosalie looked up and Gwen noticed the perspiration on her upper lip.
"I'm not feeling too well," she said. "I think I'll just go to the bathroom." She got up hastily, knocking her chair over as she did so. Her cheeks burned with embarrassment, and her eyes darted back to where Matthew sat.
He stared back and Gwen now had the excuse to follow Rosalie's line of sight. He was a very handsome man, Gwen decided, with his black hair and brown eyes, and he looked as surprised as Rosalie was. They stared at each other for a moment, before Rosalie went to the toilets. Gwen wished she could say she went with dignity.

Rosalie looked at herself in the mirror and added some eyeliner. God! Why did she decided not to come out without make-up on or brushing her hair? He was sitting there looking at her, all cool and collected, while she was sweating and panicking like a small piglet. Take it easy, she told herself; after all, he hasn't called you so he should be worried that he's going to get a mouth full. But Rosalie knew that she wouldn't say anything to him. It had been one hell of a week. Merlin was going nicely for Mary and making Mary look like she had a clue how to ride. She knew it shouldn't, but it grated on her that bad riders looked good. Neus had gone again, which always left her feeling blue; she'd had a massive fight with Jack after yet another attempt to "sin" her (as he so charmingly put it). She had resorted to throwing teabags and coffee jars at him at one stage. Then Gwen was asking her out to dinner, which was nice in theory, but getting dressed and behaving like a lady wasn't something Rosalie had wanted to do. But she had, and then Matthew turned up! It just wasn't her week.

She looked at her reflection, now aided with eyeliner. She wished she had brought her make-up bag, but of course with her luck, she hadn't. She supposed she could be grateful for finding this eyeliner, which was about four centimetres long and blunt. She put her bag over her back and walked out of the door, where she came face to face with Matthew. They were both silent.

"So, um, hi," he eventually said, clearing his throat and looking awkward.

"Hello," she answered back.

"How are you?"

"I'm fine. Thanks. Yourself?"

"Oh, you know, the usual."

"Oh, right."

They were both silent again, looking everywhere apart from each other. It irritated Rosalie. He had waited for her outside the toilets, and now he wasn't saying anything.

"Are you stalking me?" she asked.

He looked confused. "Um, no."

"Well, what do you want to say to me?"

"Nothing in particular."

"Then, why wait for me?"

"Jesus, what is this?" he snapped.

Nothing ventured, nothing gained

"Excuse me?"

"Why are you investigating why I want to talk to you?"

"Well, I'm curious because there hasn't been a word from you all week." Damn! She fumed; she hadn't wanted to bring that point up. Although she was curious why he hadn't called her or visited her, even to take the piss about what had happened. He suddenly smiled his smile and she felt her knees go week, then she felt disgusted with herself that she could still melt as soon as those straight teeth were shown.

"What?" she asked when he continued to smile.

"I wasn't aware that you wanted me to call."

"I didn't. I don't," she corrected. "God, you're just...."

"Despicable?" he offered, quoting her from that night at the restaurant. She narrowed her eyes and a grim line set to her mouth.

He just smiled back at her, adding more fuel to the fire which was burning hot and fast inside her.

"Look," he said as the smile dropped from his face and his eyes looked sincerely into hers. "I am sorry about not contacting you. I did go to Acorn stables to see you but you..."

"Don't make excuses," Rosalie interrupted.

"I'm not." He took a step towards her. "I came up to see you, but you were having an argument with a guy."

Rosalie cringed. Damn! He'd heard her insane and frantic fight with Jack. She silently pleaded with God to not let it be the one where she threw something at him.

"Then, well, I heard a crash and decided it was best to come back another day," Matthew continued.

Oh double damn, she thought, and then he went off me because I'm more trouble than I'm worth. Not that Rosalie could blame him: if she were him, she would have said bye-bye ages ago. She looked up at him, her brown eyes glistening in the light from the neon sign above them, biting her bottom lip anxiously.

"That wasn't one of my better days," she said

"Well, thank God for that, because I'd hate to see you on a bad day."

"So, what now?" she asked.

"I suppose we go back to our elders and I'll meet you out in the town centre in about ten minutes," he said with a wolfish grin. She hit him playfully.

"We can't ditch them."

"Ever heard of excuses?"

"Yes. But I won't do that to Gwen."

"Because you're a good girl?" he teased.

She laughed. "I've changed my ways. If you'd met me a while back, you wouldn't have wanted to know me."

Matthew sensed some truth in that statement, because Rosalie looked down after she'd said it. He wondered what she had been like and if what she said would have been true. But, he reminded himself, he knew this Rosalie, not the past one. He only hoped he could get to know her better.

"Well, then I'll call you."

"You do that," she said as she walked back towards Gwen. Gwen surprised Rosalie as she

Nothing ventured, nothing gained

picked up her bag and stood up.
"What's going on?" Rosalie asked.
"My lord! I forgot Sucker and he hasn't been out, poor boy."
Rosalie rose too. "Don't worry, I'll come with you."
"No, no dear, you stay here and finish your meal. I'll be round the cottage later to see you."
"Seriously, I'll come," Rosalie insisted.
"I'm going to pop into Townlands hospital while I'm here as well, to see my old friend who's ill."
"Oh." Rosalie sat down again. "Anyone I know?"
"Hmm? No Rose, but she's rather formal and doesn't like not looking her best."
"I understand," Rosalie said.
"I'll be around later. Love you dear," Gwen said as she breezed past Rosalie and out into the town square.
Rosalie looked down at her food and sighed, and then her eyes happened to look over to Matthew who was sitting alone as well and looking back at her. She raised her eyebrows as he came to sit at her table.
"I've been ditched!" he wailed in mock horror.
"Same."
"They have no respect for our generation."
"You're absolutely right! I mean, we take them out for a meal, and then they have no manners and leave! Quite monstrous."
"They remind me of when I was fifteen," Matthew said wistfully.
"Yeah, me too. Although, I did have manners."
"Sure."
"Yes, I did," she insisted.

"Of course. Want to get out of here?" Matthew asked after a second.
"Yes, please."
"Are you still hungry?" he asked as he held her coat up for her, smelling her familiar, sensual smell.
"I am. But for a kebab."
"Kebab?"
"Yes. Have you ever had a kebab?"
"Course, who hasn't?"
"You just don't strike me as a kebab character," she said as they stepped outside into the May weather. She was happy it was lighter in the evenings, it reminded her of holidays abroad, as if everything was just waking up again.
"I've done things that would shock your innocent mind."
"Hey, my mind was corrupted a long time ago."
"Would I be right in assuming that a boy tried to corrupt you?" he asked, laughing as Rosalie's face turned to him with her mouth hanging open.
"You know, you're a strange person."
"I'm not strange, I'm different."
"Well, your different personality confuses me. You seem like a gentleman and all very prim and proper, but then you say comments like that."
He was silent for a minute as they walked to the kebab stand in the car park.
"I suppose I was brought up to be prim and proper, but I'm not deep down, so they both get kind of mixed up."
"Yeah, well, I'm definitely not prim and proper."
"What are you then?"

Nothing ventured, nothing gained

They both ordered their kebabs and waited.
"I guess I'm....I don't know," she said with a small smile.
Matthew paid for their kebabs and they walked back to the town centre.
"Well, you like horses," he said.
She laughed. "I do."
"You like trespassing on people's land."
"No, not everyone's, only yours."
They both sat down on a bench.
"OK. You like throwing things at men. Hey!" he said when she thumped him one on the shoulder.
"You love your brother," he said seriously.
"My brother is my best friend. Apart from Gwen of course."
"You like.... Talking with me?" he grinned.
"No, I like teasing you, there's a difference."
"As there always is and you always like to correct and point out the differences with things."
"Can't help it if I'm naturally smart," she said as she stretched out on the bench.
"You like to think of yourself as smart," he pointed out, taking a bite of his kebab.
"You'd be surprised at how smart I am."
"You have faith."
"What? In religion?" she asked, confused. He looked at her.
"No," he laughed. "In yourself, in life, and I get the feeling that you believe that everything will work out for itself."
She was quiet. "Well, I didn't this week."
He turned to look at her, his brown eyes shining. "No, I don't suppose you did." He turned away

again and bit his kebab; Rosalie bit hers too and chewed quietly. The birds sang goodnight to their families and friends, the lights came on in the restaurants around the town centre and Rosalie saw the teenagers beginning to come out to play.
"About Robin," Matthew began, polishing off his kebab with a massive bite and throwing the wrapper in the bin next to him. "I don't know if you knew where I was going with that proposition the other night, so I'll say it again."
"OK," Rosalie said, turning her body towards him.
"You see, she needs somewhere where no one will recognise her and where I can keep an eye on her. I thought Henley was the best bet. There's nowhere for her to live in Kevin's price range, and I obviously can't have people knowing that she's living with me, as it will harm my reputation that I knocked up the heiress to the Lotte empire."
"And that would hurt your clients' reputation," guessed Rosalie.
He nodded. "Precisely. Now, I've seen your cottage and it looks pretty secluded and comfy."
"It is," Rosalie said, beginning to know what he was getting at.
"And you don't have a very high-pressured job where people are on your back the whole day."
"Well, for your information, being a waitress and working at Acorn stables is a lot harder than you think. Everyone is always watching what you do, making sure you do it right, and if you don't, you either get told off or bitched about behind your back!" Rosalie finished her kebab. "So, Mr Matthew, do not think I don't know what stress and

Nothing ventured, nothing gained

pressure are all about," she finished with a prim head nod.
He smiled at her silliness. "Forgive me. I shouldn't have assumed."
"You're forgiven," she said.
"Thank you. Anyway, what I was saying or was going to offer, was that maybe Robin could stay with you, until she feels ready enough to come clean with her father, and she could just stay in the cottage."
"What would I get in return?"
"You and your riding friends can ride on my land whenever and however you want. Just not up to the house," he warned. Rosalie considered the options. Having a stranger in the house was a violation of privacy, and she couldn't assume what Neus would say about it. But Acorn stables did need Maybrew's lands to ride on. Just the other day, there was a woman killed riding her horse on the roads, and Rosalie wasn't one for always being aware. Plus, if Robin did stay, she would have a connection to Matthew. Rosalie hated the fact that this last reason played a vital part in her answer.
"Well, I'll have to check with Neus, but if he agrees, then I think it should be fine."
Matthew's face lit up with a smile that stole Rosalie's breath away. It wasn't a sexy smile, or a flirty smile, it was a genuine happy smile.
"Excellent! You have no idea how many problems this solves."

Down he road, Beth and Gwen looked

around the corner one last time. They were both all smiles as they saw their two children sitting and smiling at each other. They congratulated themselves with a pat on the back. Their plan had worked.

Nothing ventured, nothing gained

Chapter eight

Robin Lotte had not been blessed with a natural beauty, but she had been blessed with a rich and powerful father. She knew which one she preferred having. She was an only child and her father Kurt had spoiled her rotten, always buying her what she wanted, taking her out to fancy restaurants, and allowing her to do whatever she wanted to do for her birthday. Robin didn't have a mother. Kurt had told her she'd died giving birth to Robin's sister, who unfortunately had died as well. He never talked about it with Robin, so she had made up her own opinions and images of her mother's death. Now she was twenty-two, Kurt thought it best for her to marry and settle down with a nice man. Even though arranged marriages were far and few between in England, it had always been the Lotte tradition. Kurt and Robin's mother had had an arranged marriage and Kurt's father as well. It seemed best that Robin should follow in those footsteps, even if she was a female. When he had proposed this offer to Robin, she had agreed, mainly because she loved to make her father happy and she had always done what he told her. But also because she wasn't naïve and knew some people couldn't afford to have faith in that eternal love everyone craves for. So she had agreed and met Count Vicro on several occasions. He had wit and charm and good manners – three things that Robin liked. He also had good looks that at first glance worked in his favour, but once you spoke to him his good looks didn't matter because his personality was enough for him to get by. Robin had thought it was unreasonable that he should have good looks as well: it wasn't a fair balance. She thought he had liked her as well, he was always kissing her hand when they bid goodnight and sometimes she saw him look at her with affection. She was in no doubt that she liked him and he liked her. Yet sometimes, she would feel insecure that it was all a fix. That maybe Count Vicro was taking advantage of her and her inheritance. She'd read about these types of cases in novels, read about them on the internet and had even witnessed it when her friend's husband had left with all rights to the money. The fact that Count Vicro also was good looking and a nice man made Robin's theory all the more real. What would he want with her? She knew she wasn't a particular pretty person, her hair was ginger and long (which she thought horrible), her nose was slightly too big for her face and her eyes were a fair distance apart from each other. She had also noticed that her eyebrows attracted attention, as they were brown and her hair ginger, it didn't look at all good in her eyes. One night, she went out to one of her friend's parties. That was where she met Kevin. He paid her attention most of the night and she was flattered. After all, her self-confidence needed boosting and he seemed to want to be the one to boost it for her. Perhaps now, when she looked back at that night, she wished it hadn't happened and only prayed that her father hadn't found out, as he still thought she was the virginal heiress she

Nothing ventured, nothing gained

had always been. Kevin had been surprised when she'd told him she was a virgin, but hadn't hesitated to make her a "woman", as her father referred to her losing her virginity.
"Count Vicro will make you a woman," he had always said to her. She knew what he meant, but now she was a woman, and she was a very pregnant woman. When she had told Kevin, he'd been stunned. He hadn't known what to say or how to act. All he did know was that he was in big trouble if anyone found out that she was pregnant with his child. When Kevin had told Robin the plan to stay at this Rosalie's house, she hadn't been sure. Would she be comfortable staying with a stranger who knew all her secrets? She hadn't had time to think about it, as Kevin insisted that the plan would work. That she would stay in a cottage, in Harpsden, in Henley with a girl called Rosalie and a man called Neus. So she agreed with what the men wanted. After all, she always had.

Rosalie was putting out the rubbish bags when Matthew pulled up in his car. She saw him pass a glance at Ed, sitting all clean and brand new in the driveway, but didn't comment.
"So, Mr Mason returns," she said.
He took off his sunglasses and looked down at her thoughtfully. Small freckles had appeared on her face since the last time he'd seen her, which was a week ago. He had spoken to her on the phone once or twice, to assure her that Robin was staying and arriving today. But apart from that, he

hadn't had time to see her.
Her hair had a few streaks of lighter brown in it, but her eyes had stayed the same dark, tempting brown.
"Have you been working out in the sun a lot?" he asked, picking a strand of hair between his thumb and forefinger and rubbing it gently between the two. Rosalie swallowed what felt like a golf ball; no, she thought, a tennis ball.
She met his eyes. "Yes, it's been hot."
"What have you been wearing?" he asked, looking down at her bare tanned legs and brown arms. He noticed that she tanned well, and put it down to her Spanish father's skin. Even before she had a tan her skin had been dark, but now it was a nice olive colour. A very sexy colour, he thought.
"Shorts, shirts, bras, knickers," she said with a dismissive wave of her hand.
"Hmmm." He dropped her hair and took a step back, warning himself that he couldn't get too close to her. He was Matthew Mason! He used women for sex and then left them, never had he wanted a serious relationship. He had learnt his lesson before. But he couldn't help it. Rosalie Rees inspired thoughts of hot Sundays, with a cool breeze coming through the window and entwined bodies lying against the crisp white sheets. Matthew shook his head. He couldn't think like this, he had to keep his mind on track and not let Rosalie's body or brown skin or brown eyes muddle his thoughts. He had to get Robin safe in the cottage and then head off to deal with Miss Boop and her problems with the photographer.

Nothing ventured, nothing gained

"Robin should be here with Kevin any minute," he said.
Rosalie frowned. He seemed flirty and then he closed down. He's more trouble than he's worth, she thought. If only she could believe it.
"OK. Well, Neus isn't back until Saturday."
"But, he's OK with it?"
"Hmmm? Oh yeah, he's fine."
Rosalie placed the bag down and walked back to the cottage, leaving it up to Matthew to decide to come in. If he does, then he's still keen; if not, he isn't bothered about me any more, she thought.
She turned around in the kitchen as he walked in and smiled secretly to herself. But obviously not that secretly, as he asked, "What are you smiling about?"
This made her smile even more. "I'm not smiling," she objected even as a grin managed to break through.
Matthew raised his eyebrows at her.
"OK, maybe I'm happy," she shrugged.
"About what?"
"I don't think you want to know," Rosalie informed him as she opened the fridge door and pulled out a beer bottle. She offered one to Matthew, but he declined.
"I do," he insisted.
Rosalie shook her head. "Really. It's nothing. Maybe it's the weather," she said after a second.
"It's Jack, isn't it?" he asked surprising himself and Rosalie. It wasn't the question, after all, it could have been a flirty question, but it was asked with anger and annoyance. Damn, thought Matthew,

she's going to think I like her now.
Balls, screamed the devil on his shoulder, you know you like her, in fact you like her so much you'd do anything for her.
He noticed she was laughing. "It isn't funny," he said tightly.
"Actually, it is."
"It is not!" he fumed.
She stopped laughing and raised a questioning eyebrow at him.
"Is he your type of guy?" he asked.
"No."
"Why not? You obviously dated him."
"I don't see how that is any of your God damn business."
"It is, when Robin is staying here and there will be strange men around."
"Man. Single man. And anyway, I'm sure Robin wouldn't mind, she might even encourage it!" Rosalie said in a stern, slightly raised voice.
Matthew took a step forward, anger shining in his eyes.
"She wouldn't encourage it because she has morals and good manners."
"And I guess you're implying I don't?"
"That's correct," he shouted, fists clenched.
"Oh, 'That's correct' is it? Well, fuck you!" she exploded.
"Nice manners you've got there."
"Jesus! You are such a bastard and a fucking hypocrite! You complain and go on about me shagging Jack and Donny!"
"Donny?" he asked, teeth grinding each other.

Nothing ventured, nothing gained

Rosalie laughed spitefully this time.

"Yes. Donny. But that's not the point. You shag everything that moves. I know all about you and your 'girls', Matt, so don't even dare come into my house when I'm doing you a favour and accuse me of anything."

They both stared at each other. Brown eyes against brown eyes, reflecting the anger they felt in both. It was a while before Matthew took a step back and began to laugh. At first Rosalie wasn't sure of what he was doing. Laughing in amusement or laughing in spite? Or even crying? But then she caught sight of his face and knew he was just genuinely amused. How? She didn't know, but then she found herself laughing with him. At the stupid argument that had sprang up from nowhere.

"So, am I your type of guy?" he asked, wiping his eyes free of tears of laughter.

She stopped laughing as well and gave a last chuckle before looking at him.

"You're not exactly my type of guy," she lied.

"Really? What is then?"

"Hmm...a fun one?" she asked, raising her eyebrows.

"I'm fun," he objected, taking a step towards her.

"Yeah? OK, what did you do last night?"

He didn't hesitate. "Had amazing sex with a model."

Even though she knew he was joking – or maybe not – her stomach churned with feelings of jealousy.

"You see," she laughed anxiously, "that is as

boring as never drinking, smoking or clubbing. I'm surprised you even managed to stay awake."

He smiled. "As it happens, it was a very exhilarating experience."

"Like, let's say, watching politics and arguing with the television?"

"Wow, you do that too?"

"No. I drink, smoke and dance."

"Well, like I said, I had sex with a model."

Rosalie made snoring sounds and laughed when Matthew tried to tickle her in the ribs.

"Actually, us arguing is rather fun," he said as he took her bottle of beer from her hand and drank some. Rosalie ignored the tingling that had started in her hand when he took the bottle away.

"Yeah. You're so bad at arguing it is amusing."

"Well, at least I don't resort to using every swear word God made."

"God wouldn't have made those swear words if he didn't want them used."

"What faith you have in God," Matthew said as he handed the bottle back.

"My faith in God has nothing to do with it. I have faith in swearing."

"You swear a lot?"

"Yes. It's an impulse. Like you hurt yourself, the first thing you say is 'Oh shit'."

"I don't."

"Bollocks!"

"So, I guess your impulse is also used when you're angry."

"Yes it is. It's also used when you're having fun."

"How so?"

Nothing ventured, nothing gained

"Jeez. You really are a square."
"I'm not a square. I'm just…." He shrugged.
"Look, I'll tell what, I'll do you a deal."
"What kind of deal?"
"Well, you take me somewhere you consider fun and exciting, and I'll take you somewhere I consider it fun and exciting."
"There have to be boundaries."
"OK. No sky diving," she laughed.
"Funny."
"Thanks. I thought so."
They stared at each other and then Matthew nodded.
"OK, Brown eyes."
"Brown eyes?" she questioned.
"Uh-huh. That's my pet name for you."
She hated how easily flattered she could become, just by him having a pet name for her. She also hated how easy it was to patter with him in conversation. They didn't have to have a serious topic, they could just talk about anything.
"I haven't got a pet name for you."
"Well, think of one," he said.
She put her finger to her chin and thought silently. She wanted one that was affectionate but fun. Brown eyes was nice, but she couldn't really call him the same because that would be stealing it.
"How about Sexy guy?" he asked, his eyes glittering with mischief.
She snorted doubtfully. "How about Square guy?"
"How about Handsome guy?" he asked, walking towards her.
"How about Arrogant guy?"

"How about Successful guy?"

"How about Ego guy?"

Matthew laughed as he stood closer to her. "How about Affectionate guy?" he said as he picked up her hand and brought it to his lips.

"How about Too sure guy?" she suggested, although his lips did wonderful things to her hand, making it tingle and shake with desire. Or maybe nerves, she thought.

"I like you, Brown eyes" he whispered into her ear, his breath on Rosalie's cheek. She didn't know if it was desire or the devil that made her lift her head up to meet his, and place her lips gently on his. It was so gentle that Rosalie had to open her eyes to make sure he was still kissing her. He was the first to venture out from the gentle kiss and parted her lips beneath his, to taste her fully. Rosalie again blamed the devil when she pushed her body against his; after all, she surely wouldn't be doing this by herself, would she? They touched tongues and Matthew sucked in a breath of excitement. This only spurred Rosalie on and gave her a bout of self-confidence she only ever got when she rode Merlin. Matthew had captivated her and she felt helpless. She gave herself up to the moment, savouring the taste of him and the way he moved his tongue against hers. Her body felt on fire, her skin itched to be touched, but his hands stayed firmly placed on her hips. Maybe he was a gentleman, she thought. Matthew knew he shouldn't be doing this, he had said to himself that Rosalie Rees was just a woman who would help him out, and he would help her out. He'd told

Nothing ventured, nothing gained

himself this past week that their relationship was to be purely platonic, and although he did find Rosalie attractive, he knew it was best if he stayed solo, just as he had done all his life. Balls, the devil on his shoulder told him, you know you want her too much to keep it cool between you two. "No, I have some willpower", he argued back. No matter what you tell yourself you can't deny that she feels good moulded to your body. Matthew pulled back from Rosalie and the devastating kiss they had shared. It was true, he loved the feel of her, and she was what a woman should feel like. Not all skin and bones, but the right shape. Curvy, he thought, looking at her with his brown eyes. Assessing her body. Damn! He averted his eyes. He had to maintain a level head. Otherwise things could get crazier than they already were. Rosalie's brown eyes looked into his and he found he couldn't hold her gaze. He couldn't bear to see the confusion and tenderness in them. He knew her brown eyes were his weakness and he was sure if he avoided them, then he would be able to get his breath back and think straight. Rosalie looked at him with concern. She wasn't sure what was going through his head, but it was serious enough for him to break away from the kiss and not look at her. Had she done something wrong? God, she thought silently cursing, he thinks I'm easy. She opened her mouth to say something, what she didn't know, but anything to break this awkward silence. Her mouth shut again, not sure what to say, or ask, or maybe even accuse.
"Um," she croaked. Matthew's face turned sharply

to hers, as if he'd forgotten she was there. She noted his eyes widen in panic or lust, but Rosalie's self-confidence said panic. He looked down at his shoes and Rosalie looked at his neck. She noticed he didn't have an Adam's apple showing and didn't have any moles. Unlike Mary, she thought, remembering her examination of her neck last month. Anger flared up within Rosalie, she was sure she hadn't done anything wrong, and as to why he pulled away from her, that was his problem and she wasn't going to stand there and be put into this awkward position. Just as she opened her mouth to tell him to go, he looked up at her and her eyes got lost in the darkness of his. They were clouded, she noted, perhaps defensive or protecting them from hers. But what could her eyes do to him? She wondered as she continued to struggle to break their gaze. His lips then curved into a small smile, which, Rosalie thought, could be mistaken for a grimace. He opened his mouth to say something and Rosalie felt her body tense at what he would say. Even if she tried to ignore the sound of tyres on the gravel outside, Matthew didn't look as if he could. He turned from her and peered out of the window to see Kevin and Robin arrive. He turned back to her, but unable to bear the silence any more, Rosalie walked out of the kitchen and to the front door. She opened it, her anger and frustration thrown into the action, and a massive gush of air hit her in the face. Putting a smile on her face, Rosalie walked out to Kevin and Robin.

"Welcome!" she said, looking at Robin, who just

Nothing ventured, nothing gained

nodded back.

"Hi again," Kevin said, giving Rosalie a shameful, obvious leer.

Rosalie ignored his eyes burning a hole into her boobs and legs and concentrated on Robin. It just antagonized her even more that a man could behave so rudely, especially when the woman who was pregnant with his baby was standing to his left!

"So, I've made the spare room up for you, it's next to mine. I figured you wouldn't want to be near Neus." Again Robin just nodded quietly.

"As us girls have got to stick together to make sure decency is left in the world," Rosalie continued, giving Kevin a deadpan stare. But Rosalie stiffened when she realised Matthew was standing next to her. He must have heard my comment and no doubt flatter himself to think it was about him, Rosalie thought as she crossed her arms across her chest, avoiding another look from Kevin. She didn't look in Matthew's direction as she picked up a bag from Robin's side and turned to walk away. When she noticed Robin wasn't following her, she irritably turned around and saw the three of them huddling close to one another, talking about their business. Rosalie was surprised to find herself feeling sad as she turned away from them and walked into the house. She thought Matthew had liked her and the fact that they had kept seeing each other was a good sign, but now she realised that he was just using her to get what he wanted. A room for Robin, as it were. Rosalie put the bag down on Robin's bed and sat down next to it. That's why he broke from the kiss, she thought while playing with her fingernail, he couldn't stand it and didn't think it were necessary now that Robin was living here. All the flirting and fun they'd shared didn't matter any more and he needn't do any of it again to butter her up. She'd agreed to his terms and he'd got what he wanted. Although she told herself it didn't matter, that the revelation of Matthew's purpose for being nice to her didn't matter, Rosalie was overcome with a desperate need to cry.

"Um," a small voice said by the door. Rosalie looked up and saw Robin.

"Yeah?" Rosalie asked, wiping her face to make sure no tears had dropped.

Robin shrugged then smiled. If Rosalie was a cruel woman she would have shied away from the display of Robin's wonky teeth, but Rosalie just smiled back, glad that she'd come up to see her.

"This is a nice room," she commented, looking around and running her fingers gently on the wall.

Rosalie looked around the small, cluttered room.

"It needs decorating. I would have done it before you arrived but it's been short notice."

"No," Robin assured her "I love it. It's so…homey. All my life I've lived in massive rooms, which aren't bad, but," she shrugged again, "it's nice for a change."

Rosalie stood up. "Sorry, I'll let you change and settle down."

"Thank you."

"Um, Neus will be back on Sunday. I'm not sure what time of day, but around then. Also, there's a

Nothing ventured, nothing gained

lady next door called Gwen, who lets herself in every now and then to drop off our washing." Rosalie rolled her eyes. "Me and Neus are so lazy. But she's very close to us."

"I'll be pleased to meet her."

"Well, I've told her not to scare you by just walking in, so she'll be knocking."

Rosalie walked to the door and then turned back.

"Are Kevin and Matthew still downstairs?"

Robin shook her head. Rosalie ground her teeth, wishing she'd never asked. She nodded and turned again.

"Thank you for letting me stay," Robin said shyly.

"You're very welcome," Rosalie answered, smiling and then walking away, before Robin saw tears well up in her eyes.

Chapter nine

"Tender" by Blur blasted out of the two speakers at opposite ends of the lounge, where Rosalie, Neus, Robin and Gwen sat. Rosalie was lounging on the floor, her back pressed up against the sofa, while Robin sat stiffly at the other end. Neus was sitting in the armchair, nursing a pint of beer, and Gwen sat at the dining room table, playing poker against an imaginary opponent.
"Come on, come on, come on, love the greatest thing that we have…" Neus sang off key and in a note of his own. Rosalie laughed at him and threw a cushion, to which he retaliated by throwing one back at her. Robin watched the scene in front of her and only felt sadness that she had never experienced the love and relationship that Rosalie, Neus and Gwen had. It was the perfect family scene, she thought miserably, as Rosalie threw a CD at Neus and Gwen laid another card down.
"Would you like a drink, Robin?" Neus offered, standing up.
Rosalie snorted. "You're an idiot. Course she can't drink."
"Actually, it doesn't hurt to have a few glasses," Gwen informed them, not looking up.
"Exactly. So stop worrying," Neus said to Rosalie.
"I'm not worrying, you twit, I'm just being concerned for our guest." Rosalie looked at Robin and smiled.
"If it's OK, I won't have a glass tonight, maybe tomorrow."
Neus looked at her. "You said that the night

Nothing ventured, nothing gained

before."

"And the night before," Gwen said, still concentrating on her game.

Robin blushed and didn't like the attention they were paying her.

"Leave her alone," Rosalie ordered, standing up as well. "She'll have one when she's ready."

"Yes," Robin said weakly. "I'll have one later."

Neus raised his eyebrows, but followed Rosalie as they left the room.

"Will you just leave her alone?" Rosalie snapped as they made it to the kitchen and shut the door behind them.

"She needs to chill out," Neus answered, getting a bottle of wine and pouring some into Rosalie's glass.

"She doesn't need to do anything. She's freaking pregnant!"

"Precisely. So for the baby's sake, she should chill."

"What? And alcohol is your answer to that?"

"Or sex."

"Jesus!" Rosalie swore, rubbing a hand across her face. "Men! You're all the same. Manipulate us women, get what you want, then run off like a blue-arsed fly." Neus shook his head. "You see, that's where you're wrong. It's not 'men' who do that; it's Matthew who does that." Rosalie eyes narrowed dangerously and Neus knew he shouldn't have said that. Apart from the fact that it was rude, he knew how much his sister was hurting inside. He could understand why she harboured that opinion of men now, he would if it was him, but he didn't think it fair to stereotype every male in the world as a manipulator, cheater or scum (and many more words Rosalie had used to describe men these past weeks).

But he reminded himself that was no excuse to be rude to his sister; after all, he loved her, didn't he? And he should be there, right? Only Neus didn't have a clue what to say or where to start. Not like Rosalie herself, who always comforted him if he was down. But how could he help if Rosalie kept her feelings to herself? She was a very private person when it came to serious stuff, Neus thought as he watched her now, clearing the kitchen and ignoring his comment about Matthew.

It had been two weeks since Matthew had been at the cottage and apart from the occasional call to see how Robin was settling in, when Rosalie always acted breezy and carefree, she hadn't spoken to him. It hurt her and angered her. She wasn't one to go around and beg to know why he hadn't called her for a more personal question, and she definitely wasn't going to call him and bring the subject up. Rosalie wasn't getting as much time with Merlin as she would have liked, as Mary was riding him every hour God sent. She knew she hadn't the right to feel jealous, but she couldn't help it. Jack was being a pain and it didn't help when Rosalie was feeling vulnerable and all she really craved was a hug. A hug from one man and he didn't seem available to give it to her.

Tili looked at Matthew as he frowned at the papers

Nothing ventured, nothing gained

on his desk. She often admired his work technique this way, looking through the jarred door, with a beam of light shining across the wooden floorboards. She knew he would never go for her, after all she was only his secretary, but it didn't stop her wondering. She noticed he had been staring at that same piece of paper for a long time. She was sure it was only a common statement or bill, so why was he paying so much attention to it?
"Tili? What on earth are you doing?"
Tili snapped upright and colour rushed to her cheeks. "Oh Beth, I mean Mrs Mason, sorry, um, I was…"
"Don't worry, I just didn't know if you were hurt," Beth said as she walked past Tili and pushed the door open gently and looked at her son.
She turned around and smiled down at Tili. "You can get home now if you want," Beth said, then went into Matthew's office and shut the door.
Tili gathered her things and turned off her desk light. She knew when she'd been dismissed.
"Matthew," Beth said gently.
His head snapped up to meet his mother's eyes.
"Yes? Sorry, were you saying something?"
"I've been talking to you for the last thirty seconds."
Matthew looked down at his desk and fumbled with a sheet of paper as he put it to one side.
"You could call her," Beth said, as he put her hand over Matthew's.
His eyes once again came to her and she could see the confusion.
"Mothers can tell this type of thing."

"What type of thing?" he asked, clearing his throat.
Beth smiled warmly. "Things to do with women."
"There's no woman," he objected, although Beth could tell from the guilty look in his eyes that there was one. Even if she hadn't played a part in trying to match him and Rosalie up, she was still telling the truth when she'd said she could tell.

It wasn't hard to tell, she mused, he's been like a bear with a sore head these past few weeks.

"So, what's the plan for July?" she asked.

"July?" he answered.

"Yes." She squeezed his hand. "It's July soon and we always do something special here."

"We do?"

"Matthew, we always hold a dinner party, usually in July, perhaps you could invite this woman…"

"There's no woman," he snapped angrily.

"OK," she said, getting up to sit in a chair opposite him. "How's Robin settling in that person's house?"

Matthew's eyes narrowed. "Fine."

"Is she settling in nicely?"

"She says she is."

Beth put on her best shocked face. "You mean, you haven't been to see her?" she asked shocked.

"No," he replied shortly.

"Oh dear…has Kevin?"

"Not that I'm aware of." His reply this time was tight.

"You must go to see how she is, I mean, if I were her and staying with strangers, I would be grateful to see a familiar face."

Matthew closed his eyes. His first thought was of

Nothing ventured, nothing gained

Rosalie and how he couldn't face seeing her. Then warmth spread across his chest and heated his body, seeing Rosalie was what he wanted more than anything. He missed her, it scared him to admit it, but he did. He told himself that he missed the company and silly conversations they'd had, but deep down he knew it was more than that he missed. He missed her smile, the way her eyes narrowed when she was angry, the way she raised her eyebrows when she was surprised or the way her eyes flashed when she was angry. God help him, her eyes were the thing he missed most. He'd told himself that he was doing the right thing, staying away, making it easier for both of them, because being together would just be so incredibly crazy during everything else going on. Matthew had also reminded himself of what happened last time he had given his heart away, how much pain and betrayal he had felt. But he knew he couldn't use that excuse any more, he had to see her, and he had to see her soon. He looked up at Beth, who had been watching her son contemplate the idea of going to see Rosalie with amusement and love.

"You're right, mother, I should go and see Robin. Just to see how she's getting on." He smiled and Beth knew that seeing Robin was the last thing on his mind.

The next morning Rosalie was at Acorn stables, throwing a stick for Sucker to fetch, when she noticed a Range Rover Sport pull into the stables. She looked at the car with envy, as Ed had once again needed new brakes and she didn't have enough money or patience to fix him. Her eyes scanned the silver body and dark tinted windows. It was a massive car, almost monstrous, and the first thing that came to Rosalie's mind was that it belonged to a gangster. Then her eyes saw who was getting out of the car and her mouth dropped open. Gangster indeed, she thought, staring at Matthew as he walked towards her. Her heart flipped over in her chest, her breath caught in her throat and her eyes bulged. A glowing sensation spread through her body, but then it disappeared and the panic set in. Should she turn away? Run away? Scream? Or face him like the brave woman she liked to think of herself? In the end, she turned quickly, picking Sucker up and beginning to walk away when she heard his familiar voice say her name. Her spine stiffened and she stood still. She heard him approaching closer, then knew he was standing behind her, waiting for her to turn around. Her neck prickled with the feeling of his eyes, staring, burning her skin, almost ordering her to turn around. I don't want to see him, she said to herself as she turned slowly and looked at him. But of course she did, she knew too, that she was a slave to her heart, which she always wore on her sleeve. She put Sucker down, who trotted off to lay in the shade, and she turned around. She smiled weakly, shakily, and she met his gaze. Nothing had changed about him of course, it had only been a few weeks, but it felt a lot longer than that.

"I didn't know if you would have heard me," he

Nothing ventured, nothing gained

said.
She looked confused and he smiled gently. "You usually, have your iPod on," he explained.
She nodded.
"How have you been?" he asked, taking a step towards her.
"Fine."
"How's Robin?"
"Fine."
"Neus?"
"Good."
"Gwen?" he asked this time, with a hint of a plea for her cooperation in his voice.
"Very well. She beat Louisa Jokinson at poker the other day."
"Good. I'm pleased."
They were both silent.
"Why do you make this so hard?" he muttered under his breath.
"Excuse me?" she asked. Then he smiled, which reminded her of the way he'd smiled in her kitchen when they had kissed. He always seemed to say something offensive, then smile, like she was the rude one. Arrogant jerk, she thought.
"I would leave you alone, but I think we made a promise to show each other what we think is fun, and I always keep my promises."
"Could have fooled me."
His eyes narrowed ever so slightly, and she knew she wasn't being helpful. But what did he expect? For me to run into his arms proclaiming undying love for him when he hasn't called me? She matched his narrowed gaze with one of her own.

"I think it's best if we forget that promise," she said.
His brown eyes darkened. "Really…" he said, more of a statement than a question.
"It's better for us not to see each other," she tried again to explain, but his brown eyes were stopping her concentration.
"Uh-huh."
"Yes. It would make it easier for both of us not to get….involved."
"I didn't know we were getting involved," he commented, a teasing glint in his eyes, but his mouth set in a straight line.
Rosalie wrinkled her nose and looked at her scuffed trainers. "Well, obviously we're not then."
Matthew seemed to think about smiling, and then the light went out of his eyes as he asked, "What do you really want?"
She thought about how to answer that. It was the question she'd been asking herself all her life. But when it came to Matthew, should she deny her feelings and really cut her nose off to spite her face? Or just be true and put her faith in him and the powerful "love" everyone always talked about having? She couldn't bring herself to say "I want you", it sounded too corny and too movie-like in her own ears and she was certain Matthew would think so to, so she decided to go around the houses to get the answer.
"I want a fairytale ending."
He rubbed his chin as he considered her answer.
"The old fairytales or the new Walt Disney ones?" he asked, putting off answering her answer.

Nothing ventured, nothing gained

She rolled her eyes. "Walt Disney."
He nodded. "Fairytales are fake."
"Their endings aren't."
"How do you mean?"
"Well, they leave...hope."
He looked at her. "Then that hope is fake."
She shook her head. "What's the point trying to be serious with you?"
"I am being serious," he protested.
She began to walk away. "Brown eyes," he called after her.
Damn that nickname! Goosebumps appeared on her skin and a tingling feeling, which she didn't want to put a name to, started a slow round of hitting her body on every vulnerable point.
"Please, don't be like this. Let's keep that promise and..."
"See where things go from there?" she supplied for him, her back still turned to him. He nodded, then said, "Yes."
She faced him then, and he noticed that she had that expression on her face. He couldn't pinpoint what it meant, but he had seen her use it when things weren't going according to plan and she was in danger of feeling sad. Maybe she was sad because he hadn't told her what every woman wanted to hear. Matthew, he told himself, you're flattering yourself. "OK. Let's see how it goes."

Neus looked at Robin sitting at the kitchen table, making a good job of pretending to read the newspaper. He sipped his coffee as she turned another page and raised her eyebrows at a headline. He laughed quietly to himself, knowing she was anxious with him in the room. He wondered why. And it was as much as a mystery to him even after he'd gone through everything he might have done to annoy her. As far as he knew, he'd been polite and accommodating. Maybe she was just a naturally nervous person, he thought as an answer to his own question. He did have to hand it to her that she was doing well. Many models he knew wouldn't have even considered keeping the baby, let alone running away so they could bring the baby up away from her father's disapproval. Gwen came through the back door and kissed Neus and Robin on both cheeks as a greeting. Neus saw Robin stiffen as Gwen went to kiss her and he thought that Robin probably hadn't ever been greeted that warmly before.

"Now, Neus, are you still coming to bingo with me tonight?"

"God forbid I miss out a bingo session," he said in mock horror.

Gwen pretended to whack him around the ears.

"You might meet someone there," she said mysteriously.

"Of course. I've had my eye on Angie Bradshaw, God, what the walking stick does to my libido," he groaned. "And that grey hair…mmm, I'm almost at the point of asking her to elope with me."

"Oh Neus, you really are a silly boy," Gwen said, as she dabbed her eyes free of humour tears. She looked towards Robin and smiled kindly.

"Would you like to come?" she offered.

Robin's eye grew wide. She'd never been to

Nothing ventured, nothing gained

bingo, she'd never played bingo. Sure, her father had talked about it in the past and had told her that her grandmother used to play.
"Well...um...," she stuttered, "I'm not a bingo player."
"Nor is Neus. He just sits there and makes eyes at the old women. The flirt," she said as she looked at him.
"I'm afraid that I might impose on your evening..."
"Nonsense! I wouldn't have invited you if I didn't want you to come."
Robin's eyes dashed between Neus and Gwen, like a scared prey being cornered.
"Um...OK," she said in the end.
Gwen clapped her hands together.
"Excellent."

"'I'm a Loser', by the Beatles."
"Hmmm....1965?"
"Yes. Come on, don't tell me you don't know any of the lyrics."
"Well, obviously the line 'I'm a loser' is in it."
"Duh."
"How do I respond to that?"
"With an affectionate smile and then a line that's in the song."
Matthew laughed as Rosalie smiled sweetly at him. Sucker walked ahead of them, running though the fences to sniff the bushes on the other side. They walked past the cross-country jumps, now covered in moss, as they both challenged each other about songs. Rosalie was sure he wouldn't beat her as she knew her songs well, but

so far Matthew had given her an answer to every question she'd asked. She looked at him and wondered how this game had started. She recalled teasing him about his sense of fun, then him asking her what she did for fun and her responding something about music. Somehow they had both been captured into the easy intimacy they shared. Rosalie knew that the air was charged and thick with desire and she liked to think tenderness, and although not even a simple hand had brushed another hand, she knew that he wanted to hold her hand, or repeat the kiss they'd shared in her kitchen.

However, he had remained the perfect gentleman and Rosalie marvelled at how easy and how comforting it was to talk to him and tease him. As if they'd known each other a lot longer than two months.

"She was a girl in a million my friend," Matthew answered, looking at her out of the corner of his eye. Rosalie's mind boggled, trying to remember that line in the song, and then she smiled as she could hear Paul McCartney singing it in her head.

"Well done. But I have a different line that maybe you should have used from the song."

"What's that?"

"I'm a loser and I'm not what I appear to be." He turned to her then, a questioning look spreading across his face. Rosalie looked back, wondering if she had quoted that line innocently or done it on purpose. But then, why had he chosen the line he'd said? The questions floated though Rosalie's head and she felt herself getting more and more

Nothing ventured, nothing gained

agitated because she couldn't read his mind and she didn't know what he was thinking. Was it really just flattering flirting? Or something deeper? His brown eyes glistened in the soft sun setting behind the fields, casting a mixture of red and orange over the sky, swirling and mixing with the very few clouds that still remained.

"Although I laugh and act like a clown," he continued, prompting her to finish the line.

"Beneath this mask I am wearing a frown," she said softly.

The bushes rattled beside them and Rosalie turned to see Sucker coming out, with holly and brambles stuck to his thick coat. She laughed and went to stroke him. Matthew remained silent, unsure whether or not Rosalie had felt all the feelings that belonged to both of them in that few seconds before. He sure had, and it left him unsettled that he didn't know if he was the only one being affected.

She turned and beamed at him, teeth showing and dimples appearing, and his heart turned over. Her radiant beauty shone so brightly, he couldn't help but stare at her.

"'The Times They Are A-Changin''" Matthew said, snapping himself out of his close scrutiny and starting to walk on.

"OK. Bob Dylan," Rosalie said. She shrugged. "And don't criticize, what you can't understand."

"OK. So, I now know that you love music," Matthew said, holding his hands up as if to surrender.

"Gosh, are you giving up on me, Mr Mason?" she

asked, fluttering her eyelashes and pouting.
Matthew laughed. "I'm merely giving you the credit you deserve, Brown eyes."
"Hmm. Well, I take it you don't want to play any more?"
Matthew looked over to the green, rich hilltops, going on for miles, leaving him in doubt whether they ever ended.
Rosalie stood beside him and took a deep breath. "It feels good doesn't it?" she asked.
He turned to look at her. "Yeah. It feels really good."

Neus looked at the young woman sitting two tables in front of him. She was young, that was for sure. Her eyes were big and wide, showing the blue iris as clearly as the blue sky. Her cheeks were flushed with a childlike excitement which lit up her blonde hair that was pulled back into a ponytail. Innocent was the first word that came to Neus when he looked at her. Like a child, he thought, as he watched her place another counter on her card, smiling at an elderly woman sitting opposite her. Maybe her grandmother, but Neus didn't think it was. Perhaps she was volunteering to keep the elders company on bingo night. He'd once considered doing that, but then the idea of listening to old women rattling on about their life wasn't what Neus had in mind for a good night.
He didn't mind coming to accompany Gwen though, as he thought it was the least he could do for her and Robin who sat silently to his left. What he hadn't bet on, though, was seeing this

Nothing ventured, nothing gained

beautiful, innocent creature sitting facing him, two tables down. She certainly was something he rarely saw in his line of work. All he knew were thin models, with drug habits, and the word innocent was the furthest thing from his mind when he met them. Gwen looked up at Neus, about to tell him she had nearly a full card, when she noticed that his attention wasn't on her or the game. She let her eyes look down at the card and smiled secretly. She knew who sat a few tables forward and she knew that Neus was looking at her.

"I'm just going to get a drink," Neus said, his eyes still glued to the woman.

"Yes, OK. Can you get me one?"

"Sure," he answered, getting up and walking across to her side of the room.

"I think someone's caught his eye," Gwen said to Robin, who just nodded, her eyes not looking up.

"Are you alright, chicken?" Gwen asked finally, placing her hand over Robin's clenched one. Robin's head snapped up at being called "chicken" and her eyes darted worriedly to Gwen's hand over hers.

"It's OK. You probably haven't experienced our type of friendship."

"Friendship?"

"Yes. Me, Rose and Neus, well, we tease each other, hug each other and call each other nicknames."

"I've never had a nickname," Robin admitted.

"I thought you hadn't."

Robin's head came up defensively. "But my father

has showed me love. I have received love," she insisted.

"Oh, I know you have. I'm just saying that our type of love is more open."

Robin remained quiet as Gwen smiled at her.

"How far are you gone?" she asked.

"About four months."

Gwen frowned "But I only thought Kevin told Matthew about this a few months back."

"He did. Two months to be exact, but by then I was already two months."

"You didn't tell him?"

Robin shrugged. "I didn't think he would be interested."

Gwen shook her head, her eyes showing sympathy.

"You went through the first two months on your own?"

"Yes."

"I haven't noticed you showing yet."

"I've been wearing baggy clothes. Although I've never been one to wear skin-tight clothes either."

"Me neither. Of course, I couldn't get a boob tube over my shoulder these days," Gwen joked, as her head fell back and she laughed.

"What about when you were my age?" Robin asked, gradually finding it easier to talk and ask questions than she had before.

Gwen shook her head. "Well, back then we weren't allowed to show any leg, knee or thigh. So I didn't really have a choice."

Robin nodded in agreement.

Gwen listened to another number being called,

Nothing ventured, nothing gained

and banged the table when she didn't have it. "I don't know why I bother coming to bingo, I never win anything."
"It's all very new to me. This game," Robin added, to make sure Gwen knew what she was referring to.
"It takes some skill. But you've nearly got a full card, so keep going."
Robin concentrated on her card again and Gwen snuck a look behind her and saw Neus watching the woman from the corner of the room. She was surprised he hadn't gone over there yet.

Neus waited for the final number to be called, and then made his way through the crowd towards the blonde woman.
"Hi," he said.
The woman looked around at the sound of his voice. "Hello," she answered questioningly, almost as if she was surprised that anyone would talk to her.
"I'm Neus."
"Um, OK."
Neus smiled. "It's your move to tell me your name."
"Oh, yes, well…" She looked flustered, looking at him and blushing. "I'm Tili."
Tili, he allowed it to sink in. God, he thought, even her name sounds sweet and innocent.
"So, do you play bingo here often?" He knew it wasn't the most original line, but what else could he say?
"No. I've been invited especially tonight. This is

Beth Mason," Tili said, indicating the woman talking to someone else.

The name sounded familiar, but Neus didn't take much notice of it as Tili was tucking a stray lock of blonde hair behind her ear.

"Oh, right, so is she your grandmother or....?"

"Oh, she's my boss's mother. But, I suppose she's a friend because she and my mother are friends, from way back in the day, and I guess I always knew her," Tili gushed, hating the way she felt anxious that this man was staring at her. She hadn't known a man to be quite so handsome, apart from Mr Mason of course, but then she knew she didn't stand a chance with him. Come to think of it, she thought, why is this man talking to me now?

"Oh, sorry, if you need an appointment to meet my boss I can set one up for you in the morning," she said, assuming he was there on business.

Neus raised an eyebrow. "I don't need to speak to your boss, thanks."

"Oh, I thought that's why you came over, to make an appointment."

He smiled. "No, I came over to speak to you."

"Oh." Another blush spread across her cheeks.

"So, whereabouts do you live?"

"I live with my mother in Hambledon. It's close to my work."

"So what do you do?"

"I'm an assistant for Mr Mason. He's a PR agent for some of the top celebrities in England," she answered, almost proudly.

Hmmm, Neus thought, she sounds like she likes

Nothing ventured, nothing gained

her boss a bit more than the job requires.
"You like your boss, huh?"
"Yes. He is a very good boss." Neus instantly didn't like him.
"Well, I think I'm being signalled to leave, but can I have your number?"
"Why?" Tili asked suspiciously.
Humour sprung to Neus's eyes. "So I can call you."
"Oh, OK. Of course." Tili pulled out a card and gave it to Neus.
"I'll call you."

"*Lion King*," Rosalie answered
"OK, fair enough."
"What about you?"
"I told you, I don't believe in Disney films."
"Come on!" Rosalie laughed, jabbing Matthew in the ribs. They were both standing in the car park of Acorn stables, and only their car and one other remained.
"Sorry."
"Jeez, I knew you were no fun."
"Disney films promote things that people are trying to beat in the world."
"Like what?" Rosalie asked, laughing because what Matthew was saying was surely too sad for words.
"Woman's rights," Matthew answered without taking a beat.
"Run that by me then, oh great Mr Mason."
He gave her a deadpan expression. "The women are always getting rescued by the princes; they

are stereotyped as the weaker sex. I would have imagined you would care about that."

"Really? Well, don't get me wrong, I care about women's rights and I want to be an equal, but come on! A Disney film is just a film made for entertainment and people analysing it like that takes the fun out of it!"

Matthew unlocked his car. "Well, let's just agree to disagree then."

"Fine. I can live with that."

"Tell me, when do you want to show me your idea of fun?"

"Any time," Rosalie answered, then thought she shouldn't have been so easy.

Matthew was about to answer when he saw Rosalie's eyes widen in panic as she looked past him and up the yard. Matthew would have looked around if Rosalie hadn't pulled him to her in a hug. She ran her hand through his hair, which he wouldn't have minded her doing if circumstances were different, but he only assumed that the man he saw with Rosalie last month was walking towards them.

"Sorry. Please help me out," she whispered into his ear.

"Lee! What are you still doing here?" asked Jack.

Matthew felt Rosalie stiffen as she heard his voice, then when she turned around, she kept her arms around Matthew's neck and pressed her body up to his side.

"Oh, we were just walking the dog."

"You have a dog?" Jack asked Rosalie, his eyes never looking towards Matthew.

Nothing ventured, nothing gained

"Well, I'm looking after him."

"You always wanted a dog. Do you remember when we played that game?"

Rosalie shook her head.

Jack laughed. "You know, about what dog we would have and what we would call it?"

Inside Rosalie fumed, because it was obvious Jack had brought that up to make Matthew uncomfortable. She would have liked nothing more than to punch Jack in the face and disfigure his perfect button nose and see his fake green eyes water.

But for now, she settled for saying, "There were a lot of things we talked about, namely your wedding that you had."

His smiled fell from his face, but his green eyes stayed on hers. "Yes, weddings are stressful," he commented

"They are," Matthew agreed, earning a look of intrigue from Rosalie. Matthew tightened his grip on Rosalie's waist and pulled her closer, making her body mould to his in an intimate way, which made Rosalie wonder if he knew he'd pulled her closer. Jack had obviously seen the not-so-subtle movement as he made his excuses about meeting Mary and left. Rosalie watched him go, then looked up to see Matthew's expression and was surprised to see him looking down at her. She smiled weakly and tried to move herself from him, but he just kept his hold tight and continued to gaze into her eyes.

"You and me need to talk, Brown eyes," he whispered huskily.

"About what?" she squeaked.
"About Jack and what he means to you." Matthew released her, but kept her close enough for her to feel his body heat.
"He means nothing."
He gazed down into her eyes for a moment longer before giving her a wry smile.
"Well, perhaps he means nothing to you now, but I would stake my life on the fact that he once meant a lot to you."
She avoided his dark gaze and she looked at her shoes. "Perhaps he did, but not now." She looked up at him. "Now he means very little to me."
"Well, you need to figure out how little he means to you, then give me a call when you're done."
"Me call you?" she asked
He smiled. "Of course. Have you got an objection to doing that?"
She swallowed. "No, not at all." Of course she had a problem with it! He was the one who was supposed to ring her; she wouldn't be doing the chasing.
Matthew opened his car door and stood looking at her. "It's just, I don't seem too good at getting into contact with you."
"No. You don't," she answered, meeting his gaze head on, letting him know that she didn't appreciate it either.
"In fact, if you're up to it some time, ride up to Maybrew and I'll meet you."
"Maybe," she answered.
He got into his car and rolled the window down. "Working class hero."

Nothing ventured, nothing gained

She smiled, remembering their game earlier. "They hate you if you're clever and they despise a fool," she answered.

"Damn," he said as he pulled out. "You know everything."

She watched him drive away and then the smile dropped from her face. "I don't know anything about you," she muttered as she put Sucker into Ed and drove away.

Chapter ten

There was a change in Matthew that Beth couldn't put a name to. As her son, she thought she knew him better than anyone, but she was stunned by the effect that knowing Rose had on him. He was whistling, smiling at everyone, singing (although tunelessly) to each song that came on the radio. Beth was still getting over the shock of him owning a radio and now playing it when he worked. He'd never really cared for music, like she hadn't, but now he listened to it religiously and smiled when a song came on, which she presumed he knew well, for he was singing and laughing to himself. Obviously Rose had something to do with it which filled Beth with happiness that Matthew had taken to this woman. Not that she doubted Gwen when she'd guaranteed he would fall in love with Rose, but the few weeks before he'd seen her again it had been touch and go. It had now been a week since Gwen had assured her that Rose and Matthew were seeing one another frequently, and she had seen Rose turn up on a massive horse the other day and Matthew went out to meet her. They had walked around the grounds together. Also, not that Beth was constantly watching the pair like a hawk, she noticed that Matthew now was putting his arm around her shoulder, or around her waist, or even giving her a hug when they said goodbye. In return, Beth had been pleased to see Rose giving him a small peck on the cheek and taking his hand. Although Beth had only noticed these displays of affections these

Nothing ventured, nothing gained

past couple of days, so she didn't want to get her hopes up too far.
She picked up the phone and rang Gwen's number.
"Hello?"
"Hello, Gwen, its Beth."
"Oh Beth! How are you?"
"I'm very well, thank you. However, I was wondering what the situation is on Neus and Tili."
"Oh, well, they are going out tonight, and Matthew is going over to Rose."
"Oh, how very pleasant."
"Yes. Oh Beth, I must ask you something about Tili."
"Oh?"
"Yes. I was wondering if you knew if she had any…experience with men?"
Beth was quiet as she considered her answer. Although Tili's mother hadn't come out and said it straight, Beth was sure that Tili hadn't had any experience.
"I don't think she has, Gwen, but I don't know for sure."
"OK. That's fine. I'll subtly mention to Neus that he should be careful with her."
"Perfect. Well, I must go to the doctor's now, so I will see you later on. Shall we meet in Café Rouge?"
"Yes. About six? I would like to bring Robin with us if that is OK?"
"That's fine. Six it is. Goodbye."
"Bye."
Beth put the phone down and sat thoughtfully. The

visit to the doctor's was a check-up, making sure she was still going strong, but she couldn't put the results off any longer. It just put everything into perspective since she'd been told at the Royal Berkshire Hospital. And although she didn't want to alarm Matthew, he did need to know.
Not now though: soon, but not now.

"Turn at A…that's good, now bend him a little bit towards the right.….left leg….no, left leg.….that's it…rise to the trot…look ahead.….head up!" Rosalie ordered, losing her patience quickly. She didn't want to be here now, in the menage, watching Mary bounce over Merlin, not listening to her instructions. She was surprised when Mary had asked her to help her out when schooling Merlin, but she'd accepted. What else could she say?
"OK, now push him into a slower trot.….rise slower….no, slower…."
Rosalie watched with dread as Mary met Merlin's bounces with a bounce of her own. She shook her head, feeling sorry for her because she really didn't have a clue how to ride. And if she seriously thought she was going to do a Novice test in the next two weeks, she was deluded. This only made Rosalie feel sorrier for her. Tonight, Rosalie was having Matt over to watch films. It wasn't her fun thing she wanted to show him, she had a much juicier one in stored for him. Which, if she knew him at all, he wouldn't think of as fun.
"OK, now come down the centre line……get ready to pull him up…gather your reins….and gently pull

Nothing ventured, nothing gained

back…gently,….GENTLY!" Rosalie's hand flew to her eyes, unable to watch Mary jab Merlin violently in the mouth. Rosalie could have sworn that Merlin's big dopey eyes looked towards her for help.

"OK, enough for today," she said brightly, smiling at Mary, being careful not to make her despondent about riding. Rosalie knew what it was like to be criticised in a harsh way. Her parents did it enough on a regular basis.

Mary dismounted and pulled her stirrups up. Rosalie made her way towards her, and then was shocked to see her eyes watering.

"Are you OK?" she asked.

"I'm f-f-fine," Mary stuttered.

"Come on now, tell me what's wrong."

Suddenly Mary's tears were released and she cried desperately, hanging on to Merlin's saddle.

"It's J-j-jack." Mary wiped her eyes. "He said I couldn't ride M-M-Merlin and that I would screw up the h-h-horse event-t."

"No, you won't," Rosalie said, feeling guilty because she had thought the same thing. But that Jack would tell her this, Rosalie thought was totally out of order.

"Just have faith in yourself."

"How can I?"

Rosalie was silent and then she smiled kindly. "In your head, just keep saying to everyone 'Fuck you'."

Mary drew in a breath, shocked at the use of foul language, but Rosalie only laughed.

"Don't tell me you don't swear either."

"Who else doesn't swear?"
Rosalie thought of Matthew, but thought it best not to mention him. She was talking and fantasising about him too much lately.
"No one. But it's OK to swear in your head. Not even God can tell that."
"The Lord knows everything. What people think, what people want to do and what people will do," Mary answered, tilting her chin up to show she was serious. Rosalie just laughed.
"So you're religious, huh?"
"Yes. I go to church every Sunday and pray every night."
Rosalie nodded thoughtfully. "Good for you."
Mary remained quiet.
"Look, don't worry, you'll get better, err, I mean you'll improve in the next week or so."
"Will you help me?"
Rosalie suddenly saw a young child, seeking reassurance from an adult, and felt her heart expand.
"Of course."

Neus looked into the mirror at his reflection. He was pleased at what he saw. Hair naturally styled, his face clean and shaven. He dressed casually, which comprised denim jeans and a white t-shirt. He hoped Tili would be pleased even though she gave him the impression that if she was, she wouldn't say so. This last week, he had got to know Tili and learnt that she was just an ordinary girl, with a good job. Although she wasn't ordinary, she was gorgeous. Yet Neus thought her

Nothing ventured, nothing gained

gorgeousness represented what was inside her. As a person she was lovely, kind, sweet and innocent. To Neus, this made everything about her gorgeous. Tonight he planned to take her to an Italian restaurant called Anticos, just a short walk away from Henley square. The food and service were to a high standard and Neus couldn't wait to see Tili's enthusiasm.

The front door slammed downstairs, followed by a line of muffled swearing. Neus rolled his eyes, in no doubt that Lee had come home and was running late. As usual.

"Lee?" he asked, walking down the stairs and finding her in the kitchen, fingers tapping impatiently against the surface of the table.

"You OK?" he asked, sitting down opposite her. She looked at him and smiled weakly.

"What do I do?" she whispered.

"Huh?"

"Like, what do I say when he comes over? I'm nervous."

Neus laughed and smiled when Rosalie frowned at him.

"You may think it's funny," she continued, fingers still tapping the table. "But I've never had a man over here. For a proper dinner date and conversation."

Neus looked at his sister and shook his head. He could understand why she was nervous, his stomach was doing all sorts of things at the prospect of taking Tili out, but he also was forced to recognise that Lee thought that this Matt guy was someone special. Of course Neus was pleased for her, he wanted Lee to be happy, but it also led to questions that he didn't want to answer. Would she move out and live with this Matt guy? Where would that leave him? Who would he have to live with? Although Neus was twenty-six, he had never been made to stand on his own. There had always been Lee waiting to catch him if he fell. She was his safety net which now, Neus discovered, had holes in it.

"Just be yourself. He'll fall in love with you."

"That's not what I want," she answered, her cheeks reddening.

"Sure," Neus said, getting up and opening a window. "Just go and get changed out of those stable clothes and out on something nice and sexy."

"Sexy?" she asked.

"Yeah. Now, as your brother this is a kind of strange thing to be advising you , but if you want advice, here it is." Neus cleared his throat. "When men are invited around the girl's"

"Woman's."

"Yeah, woman's house for dinner, he thinks she's gonna sleep with him. This is true in many cases."

"Percentage?" Rosalie asked.

"Hmm, about ninety-five per cent."

Rosalie gulped as Neus continued speaking. "So, he is coming over with that in mind. He's going to be as charming as possible, ask all the right questions and compliment you."

"He is?"

"Yes."

"But what if I don't want to sleep with him?"

Nothing ventured, nothing gained

"Well, then you say that, straight away though, so you can test his character. If you say that and he just laughs and says fine, but still stays, then you know that wasn't his sole purpose for coming. If you say that, then he gets a 'phone call', then you know that was all he wanted."
Neus looked at Lee's troubled face. He didn't feel big or good about what he was doing, and he knew it was childish and selfish, but the sudden rush of loneliness that washed over him was aching to be soothed over with reassurance. This way, Lee wouldn't want this Matt guy coming over, and she would have to come out with him and Tili. But as he watched her face, he saw her eyes shining with what looked like humour.
"If he does that I will punch him!" she declared jokily and stood up, ready to go and get changed.
"Do you still want him to come over then?"
"Of course. I can't back out now and anyway," she shrugged, "he isn't like the other ninety-five per cent of the male population." She patted Neus on the shoulder as she passed and went to her bedroom.
After a few minutes, Neus got up and walked to the door. He shouted goodbye to Lee and went to his car. It appeared that this Matt guy meant too much to Lee already, so much that she had just ignored her brother's advice.

  Rosalie screwed up her face as she looked at the lounge. It was dusty, dank and smelt of last night's cigarettes. She needed to tidy up, but didn't have time. Instead, she settled for opening the windows, pushing the curtains back so light came in, gathering the bottles and ashtrays and putting them in the kitchen. She hadn't planned anything for dinner; she assumed they would get a takeaway. After all, she wasn't going to change for Matthew and she definitely wasn't going to be something she wasn't, and a cooking-happy housewife was not on her list of things to be. Neus's advice had done her good. It reminded her that she was what she was and Matthew would have to deal with that. Whether or not she slept with him tonight was something she would decide later, and if he did get a 'phone call' then it was goodbye Mr Mason. Rosalie got out the takeaway menus, pizza, Chinese, Indian among others, and set them on the table. She had been so engrossed in looking at the pizza menu that she hadn't heard Matthew's car pull up. It was only his knock on the door that brought her back to reality. A shiver ran down her spine. How did a man like Matthew manage to be the cause of shivers, stomach flip-flops and her heart beating faster than ever before? She opened the door and looked at him. He wore black jeans and light cream top. She hadn't seen him in jeans before, he was always in suits, but now she had, it was hard not to let her mind run amok with thoughts that gave her great pleasure. He looked at her as well, but she couldn't quite pinpoint his expression. Perhaps between amused and flirtatious, or serious and stunned – he was that hard to read.

"Hey," he said, stepping into the cottage as Rosalie stepped back. "How are you, Brown

Nothing ventured, nothing gained

eyes?"
Rosalie wished that his nickname for her didn't flatter her quite so much.
"Fine. Yourself?" she asked, closing the door behind him. She turned to him, assuming he had walked ahead into the kitchen, and smacked into his chest as her knees bumped against his.
"Ooof," she grunted. She couldn't say anything else because her breath had been knocked out of her. They looked at each other. Neither of them made to move apart. Like her brain had been disconnected from her body, she placed her hands on his broad chest, as if to him push away, but only left them there and felt his chest rise with quickened breath. She pictured the following scenes in her head. Him bending his head to kiss her, she kissing him back with hunger, then him picking her up in his arms and carrying her upstairs where he laid her down on her clean sheets and….
She snapped herself out of her daydream and smiled sheepishly. She stepped back, allowing her hands to drop from his chest, and she wasn't sure if she had imagined the look of disappointment flicker in his handsome face.

Tili was nervous. Oh sure, she had been out on dates before with young men, although they were never as good looking as Neus and didn't have as much money as Neus did, and also didn't have a dazzling smile that made her heart flutter. Like Neus did. Tili thought of Matthew and then discarded him from her thoughts. She wouldn't think about him. Although he had been kind to her and even joking with her these past few weeks, she was still wary of him. With Neus she felt safe and comfortable.

She looked at his smile, open and inviting for her to kiss his lips. Tili mentally fanned herself. She had never been this attracted to anyone before, with the exception of Matthew she had never thought she could feel this way. But, she reminded herself as she sipped her wine, Neus was available, Matthew wasn't. She dared herself to touch his leg under the table, or reach across the table for his hand, but she didn't. She was nervous he would pull away or look at her with disgust. She had read the Jackie Collins novels and read the magazines, and she knew what to do and what not to do. And as a woman, she should allow him to do the chasing; she should be strong and be powerful, because that's what men found attractive. She should be like Lucky Santangelo. But what did confuse her was, if she was supposed to be powerful and in control, then shouldn't she grab his hand? Show him she meant business? She nodded to herself as she looked at Neus as he spoke about his modelling jobs. She would reach her leg out in a minute and touch his. He would then smile and touch hers back. Just like in the films and books. She attentively stretched her leg out a few centimetres towards his. Her hands clenched as she stretched her leg further and felt it connected with another leg. She smiled and looked anxiously at Neus, looking for a reaction. There proved to be none. She bit her lip.

Nothing ventured, nothing gained

OK, he was playing this cool. She could do that.
She lifted her leg so she could raise her ankle and brush it along his.
"So, I do modelling just for the cash. I don't need handouts from my parents, I have pride but..." He continued talking, apparently not taking any notice of her ankle brushing.

But wait! Someone was applying pressure back on hers. She smiled, finally deciding that Neus was playing a game to make the atmosphere and touching even more erotic. She understood about the games some men liked to play to intensify their need. Neus must be one of those men. That's OK, she told herself, she didn't mind catering to his needs; after all, he was gorgeous and she really did feel aroused at the prospect at playing this game. They continued to talk, Tili applying more pressure and casually sliding her ankle all the way to his knee, then slowly down again as if to allow him to imagine how she would repeat that action with another limb. In return, he applied more pressure as well, but didn't move his ankle any higher. She wondered if that meant he wanted her to be in control, and as she was taking on that attitude, she didn't mind in the least taking the lead. Neus kept on talking as if their game wasn't happening, and she was a little intimidated that he could act so casually when she knew what effect it was having on her. She excused herself to go to the loo, needing to rethink her situation. She decided that maybe it was better not to carry on with the game and let him come to her if he wanted more foot play to continue.

As she turned towards the table a man blocked her way. She tried to step left, but he followed, then right and he blocked her that way too.

"Can I help you?" she asked pleasantly.

"Come on, we can go in here," the man said as he grabbed her hands and pulled her towards the back door which led to the alleyway outside.

"Excuse me?" she demanded, stopping and pulling her hands away. The man's face turned red with embarrassment, but then relaxed as he smiled. He really was an ugly man. Not her type at all. He had buck teeth, a massive Adam's apple that bobbed up and down with his swallowing and his breath was in dire need of a mint. Not to mention his beer belly and the not so flattering t-shirt that was tucked into his too-small jeans.

"Don't play the innocent with me. I've got such a hard-on and I'm waiting for you to deflate it for me," he gushed, as his eyes moved from side to side.

Tili grimaced at his choice of words and tried to walk past him again. But since he blocked her, she stood her ground.

"I'm sorry that you are in a desperate need of….release," she cringed as she said it. "But I am not the person to help you with it, I don't even know you and it is rude for you to suggest I do help you."

The man's face turned angry. "You prick tease, you rub my ankle and leg all night, wanting me to feel all worked up so you can put me down at the last minute?"

Tili's face turned white. He was the ankle player?

Nothing ventured, nothing gained

"And to be honest I feel sorry for the guy you're with because he's in for a hell of a surprise. You stupid little bitch."

"Hey," said a voice behind them, which turned out to be Neus as he stepped forward.

The man smiled. "Just saying that you have your hands full here, mate. She's a fucking prick-tease and a whore."

"How dare you?" Neus asked, as he suddenly turned angry too.

The man turned from Tili to Neus, as Neus walked forward so they were nose to nose.

"Yeah, I dare mate, what are you gonna do about that huh?" Then out of nowhere, the man grunted as Neus's hand made contact with his face.

The man went down, taking a waiter with him who had came out to see what was going on. The man got up and lunged at Neus, catching him directly in the stomach and sending him back against the wall.

"Shit!" exclaimed Tili as she watched the two grown men scuffle on the floor, pulling each other's hair and biting their ears. There was various grunting from them, some swearing and cries of agony. The man got up and stumbled to his feet, breathing hard and wiping his face. Neus rose too and they looked at each other; they both began to lock horns again. Waiters intervened and tried to pull them apart, but that wasn't necessary as the man got a lucky punch and sent Neus flying into the trolley of freshly made desserts, all falling over and landing on Neus's body. The man got up and ran to the front door, leaving whoever he was

with behind.
Tili went over to Neus and looked down at him. She was afraid he would be angry and was delighted when he sat up, cheesecake smudged all over his face, smiling broadly.
"That was as much fun as I've had in a long time," he said with a grin.
Tili laughed, thankful that he saw the funny side of it, and then laughed even more when he picked up a strawberry tart and pushed it into her face.

"Favourite film?" Matthew asked, sipping his wine and looking down to where Rosalie was lying on the floor. They were both full after their Chinese takeaway, and debating what film to watch while they drank their drinks. Rosalie was sticking to vodka and coke because it didn't go to her head quite so much as wine did, and the last thing she wanted was to end up declaring undying love and scaring Matthew off. He was sticking to wine, but she didn't dare ask if that was his safe drink or risk drink. She didn't have the courage.
"Hmmm. I don't have a favourite film," she answered, rolling onto her belly and looking at the DVD rack. Matthew tried not to stare at the bare skin showing between her top and the waistband of her jeans, but he was only a man and Rosalie was an incredibly attractive woman.
"There must be a few that you really like though," he pointed out.
Rosalie tapped her lips with her forefinger, as if to consider his question. "I suppose. But, there are all different types of moods, aren't there?"

Nothing ventured, nothing gained

"Huh?"

"Well, if you're in a sad mood then you'd watch something like….*Titanic*. Or if you're in a happy mood, a romantic comedy would be the one to watch."

"What about a scary film?"

"Well, I guess that you'd need to be in an I'm-not-scared mood," she said with a grin.

"OK, so what mood are you in now?"

"Hmm. Tricky question."

Matthew smiled and put down his wine as he went to sit on the floor next to Rosalie. Together they looked at the DVD rack and picked out films that neither of them would turn their nose up at or make jokes about.

"We need to make a decision," Matthew commented as Rosalie discarded yet another DVD in the reject pile.

"Yeah," she replied, picking up her drink. "I guess so, otherwise it's gonna get too late to watch something."

"Past your bedtime?" he teased.

"No, I was just thinking of all those political programmes that you're missing making notes on."

"I suppose, or I'll keep those models waiting my phone call that would make their day."

"Jesus, could your head get any bigger?"

"Dunno. Want to try it?"

"Uh-oh."

"Why does making my head bigger have to be something bad? You could enjoy it."

"Well, I guess it would be bad because everything

about you is bad."
"Really?" he asked, flattered.
"Not in a flattering way."
"Women sometimes tell me that I'm very bad," he drawled in a low, seductive voice.
"Well, no offence…"
"None taken," he interrupted.
"But the women you date don't really talk a lot of sense."
"Wow. That's harsh. Look, I know you're jealous but there's really no need to be bitchy."
"Jealous of you and your bimbos? Hah!"
"What 'hah?'"
"That unbelieving 'hah' that I use when your massive ego and arrogance rise to the surface. You just assume I'm jealous when really I'm repulsed by all the women you've dated. God! Dyed blonde hair and no doubt they dye their pubes as well! Even their bloody leg hair!" she exclaimed, instantly embarrassed and appalled by her outburst. Lord help her, she was jealous and she had just made it completely obvious.
Matthew remained silent.
"You could have just said that you weren't jealous," he eventually said.
She sighed. Yes she could have, and now she was kicking herself because she hadn't.

Nothing ventured, nothing gained

Chapter eleven

Gwen looked at Robin, her face expressionless as she watched Robin cower under her gaze. Beth looked from one to the other, hoping to God that Gwen hadn't heard or didn't understand what Robin had allowed to slip out. Not only that, but Beth was fuming inside that Kevin had told her anything to do with Matthew.
"Excuse me?" Gwen asked.
Robin's eyes darted nervously between Gwen and Beth, unsure of what to say. Beth's expression didn't give her any clues. Should she continue? Or make a joke and move on to another conversation?
"Robin," Gwen said, but to Robin it sounded like a warning, or a threat. She gave Beth one last glace before turning to look at Gwen.
"I just said that Kevin told me that Matthew was married."
Gwen's hand flew to her chest. She hadn't expected anything to come out of asking Robin to repeat what she had heard while coming back from the loos.
"Married?" she uttered, looking at Beth, who remained silent, staring back at Gwen.
"Why didn't you tell me? Why bother setting him up with Rose if he already had a wife?" she demanded, her face now going hot with anger.
"He isn't married any more," Beth replied calmly, looking at Gwen then Robin.
Robin's face went red with embarrassment.
"Oh, Kevin told me that he was…"

"Kevin has his facts wrong. And before you go telling everyone, Robin, I suggest you get your own facts right."
Beth turned to Gwen. "Matthew used to be married to an Irish woman called Carmen. They are not married any more."
"But surely you should have told me beforehand."
"Why? What difference does it make?"
"Well, if the marriage ended because Matthew had an affair or he beat her or something, then I think I should have known, otherwise I wouldn't have got Rose involved."
"Why do you assume the marriage ending was Matthew's doing?" Beth asked.
"Wasn't it?"
"Well, as a matter of fact, it wasn't anything to do with him. Carmen ended it."
"But why?"
"Does it matter?" Beth asked.
"Yes."
"I'm sorry," she said shaking her head. "I'm not about to discuss my son's marriage when it has nothing to do with his relationship with Rose. He has treated her nicely, as a lady, and she seems to have fallen for him as he has for her. Therefore, I do not think past details are important." With that Beth got up and left the table, leaving an open-eyed Gwen and Robin staring after her.

"It's only nine," Tili said as she and Neus walked into her house.
"Yeah, I thought time flies when you're having fun."

Nothing ventured, nothing gained

"No, it doesn't. Each moment is long enough to savour," she said with a giggle.
"Is your mum home?"
"No, she's gone out to bingo, I think," Tili answered, turning on the lights even though it was still reasonably light outside. She felt arms wrap around her waist and her neck tingled from the light touch of Neus's lips. Did she turn around now? Wrap her arms around his neck? Or stay like this? So many questions rushed through her mind that she felt dizzy.
Neus kissed her neck once again, lightly. Tili turned, trying to be graceful like she saw on the movies, but managed to catch the side of Neus's head as her arms flew out at the sides.
"Shit!" he cursed, grabbing his temple and rubbing it.
"I'm sorry," she gushed, removing his hand and rubbing his head for him. "I was....um...trying to turn around..." She trailed off, suddenly unsure whether he would want to know.
He smiled, and then winced as the pain settled in. "Don't worry. It will wear off after a while," he said, and taking her hand he brought it to his lips. Her stomach dipped low as their eyes met and she was wrapped into the most gentle kisses she had ever experienced. Not that she had experienced many. Tili had never been the popular girl who went out and got drunk and ended up necking with guys in the darkened corners, she hadn't really ever seen the point.
"I don't have much experience," she confessed as they broke apart.

Neus's mouth went dry. She was a virgin! This gorgeous creature, who was in her early twenties, was a virgin. This wasn't good, he thought as he backed away.

"Well, maybe you should be sure...," he started, and then stopped. He couldn't really imagine himself leaving this house tonight without having slept with her. She was so pretty and she got his juices running higher than any woman had before.

"Oh, I am sure," Tili replied.

Neus grinned as Tili noticed a teasing glint had appeared in his eyes. Her face was a picture. Slightly scared, although curious why Neus was grinning so much. He grabbed her with an urgent tenderness and pulled her towards him, pressing her closer to his body so she could feel him everywhere. Tili gasped as she felt his hardness and wondered if this was how sex was nowadays. Did men just grab you and pull you to their bodies? The first time she'd had sex she had been with Jimmy Bosh, her boyfriend of five years. The fun they had had! He had been so gentle, until they'd discovered new things together. But she had never been grabbed and pulled. Tili decided to go along with it and see what Neus's next moves were; after all, she was keen to learn.

Neus kissed her, anchoring her head in his palms to allow his tongue to slip between her parted lips. He explored her mouth with obvious curiosity and was pleased to feel her respond to him by running her hands down the sides of his body and through his hair.

Neus pulled her top over her head, getting it

Nothing ventured, nothing gained

caught on her earring and making her scream.
"Shit, I'm so sorry," he panted.
Tili rubbed her ear and tried to smile.
"That's OK," she said, and then she smiled more brightly as Neus looked at her chest and gave a low wolf whistle. He reached around and unclipped her bra, letting it fall to the floor.
They kissed as they made their way over to the sofa in the lounge. It was there Tili unbuckled his belt and pulled it from his trousers. She snapped the top two buttons and slid the zip down. Neus groaned and closed his eyes when Tili touched his hard penis.
For a minute Neus's mind was boggled, he couldn't think beyond the feeling of Tili's dainty hands on him, but then after a few minutes, he looked down at her and saw the look of concentration on her face as she looked at his penis.
"Tili?" he croaked.
She looked up at him, holding his penis in her hands.
"Sorry, I was just checking," she explained.
"Checking?" he asked.
"Yes," she replied, looking back down and pulling his penis to either side and inspecting it closely.
"For what?"
"I was just checking that you don't have, like, genital warts or herpes. Anything like that."
Tili wasn't sure if it was her, but she began to feel him grow soft.
"What's wrong?" she asked, getting up from her knees and looking at Neus's pained expression.

"You can't say things like that," he said.
"Why not?"
"Why not?" He sighed, pulling his trousers up. "It….spoils the mood. It makes the moment stop." He snatched his shirt up angrily and Tili cowered away.
"It's just, after so many years with one man, I need to make sure that I don't catch anything."
"Do you think I'd have sex with you if I had anything?"
"Well, you might not have known."
"Believe me, if there were…warts," his face screwed up at the thought, "I'd know."
"Do you check yourself regularly?" she enquired, reaching for her shirt too, because the mood had been completely ruined.
Neus stared at her, dumbfounded. "What do you do in your spare time? Offer people advice on sexually transmitted diseases?"
"Of course not. You can't blame me for being concerned for my health."
Neus was suddenly angry. "Well, what else were you looking for? Huh? Could you somehow tell if I had Chlamydia? Or the clap?"
Tili narrowed her eyes, not liking Neus's tone. "If you have a problem with me checking your penis for these things, then you're not worth it," she said moodily, stomping into the kitchen.
A few minutes later she heard the front door slam. Maybe Neus wasn't the one, she thought as she put the kettle on.

"OK, give me your favourite film which is a light

Nothing ventured, nothing gained

hearted one," Rosalie said, returning the conversation to its original point.
"You first."
"*Pretty Woman,* and for a dark type of film, I guess *One Flew over the Cuckoo's Nest.* You go now."
"Um, dark one probably *The Green Mile*, and for a light one…I dunno," Matthew said with a shrug as he looked at Rosalie who was sitting at the other end of the sofa. The sofa wasn't massive, but Rosalie had brought her legs up to her chest. Matthew didn't know if this was a self-defence mechanism or purely for comfort.
"Don't have time for light-hearted films?" she asked lightly
"Well, maybe *The Green Mile* is the light-hearted one," he smiled.
"You must be joking."
"Thought you believed I couldn't be fun or funny."
"I have to put it to the test."
"How?"
Rosalie tapped her nose and stretched out her legs in front of her.
"I know a way to have fun," Matthew said mysteriously.
It was only when Rosalie turned to look at him that she knew what type of fun he was talking about. "I told you I'm Catholic: sex is a sin."
"So get stuck in?" he finished for her.
"Hah!"
"Jesus, not that 'hah' again," he said with a sigh as he put his glass down and sat on the edge of the sofa. He turned to look at her, so he was instantly closer. But not for comfort, she thought as a flare

of desire and arousal shot through her body.

"Anyway, you need stamina," she said with a gush of breath that she would have preferred him not to have heard.

He just smiled as if he knew what she was experiencing.

"I have that. In fact," he said, moving closer, "I can do anything to a woman."

Rosalie laughed nervously and looked towards Sucker, as if for help. Unfortunately, all Sucker did was open one lazy eye, look at her, and then close it again.

"What would you do, Sucker?" she asked.

"Sure. I'd be prepared to suck her," Matthew replied, smiling.

Rosalie looked at him with eyes narrowed.

"One-track mind," she said.

"And you love playing that track over and over again," he commented as he lifted his finger and trailed it in light circles around her knee.

Rosalie looked at his finger, then at him. "That track is so old, it's battered."

"Yet, regardless of the hesitations, jumps and screwed-up lyrics, it still speaks to that emotion," he said wistfully.

"Yeah, anger, boredom."

"More like love, happiness."

"If you think you have anything to do with my emotions then you are deluded."

"Well," he said, running his finger a little higher towards her thigh now, "at least it's safe to say I make you angry."

Rosalie sighed and Matthew grinned. "And you do

Nothing ventured, nothing gained

love my tracks."
She looked into his eyes and noted that there was an element of a challenge mixed with the arousal she was feeling. Well, she was never one to back down from a challenge, even if she knew this challenge would lead her somewhere which was wrong, but where she so desperately wanted to go.
"I wouldn't go near your tracks," she said, raising her chin higher.
If Matthew felt any surprise that she was carrying the conversation on, then he didn't show it as he said, "But you want to go near my tracks and my drumstick."
"If you brought you track or your drumstick anywhere near me I would happily make sure they never played a tune again."
"That's OK, I'm perfectly happy watching you play your triangle."
Rosalie's eyes narrowed and her insides melted as she thought of what he was suggesting. "Oh please," she said, stuck at what else to say.
"If you keep begging, I'd seriously think about bringing my pick out too."
"What, and play it as I made a tune with my triangle and recorder?" This time the surprise showed on his face as his eyebrows rose and his mouth curved into a smile.
"No greater pleasure."
"Yeah, but I've seen many instruments before, especially picks and drumsticks, and they're all very boring. Yours would be no exception."
"I've trained with them for years," he insisted. "And

the tunes I create sometimes get a round of applause."

"Well, they won't from my triangle and recorder."

"I don't know if you could help the applause just…coming." His voice grew low and soft as he said the last word.

Her eyes opened wide and she looked into his. The fire that had been bubbling up inside her was now in full swing and the heat between her legs had intensified so much that if Matthew didn't make a move in the next minute, she would be forced to jump him.

"It wouldn't come just off its own back, it'd need working on, and I'm sure your drumstick and your pick aren't up to the job."

"How do you know if you don't try?"

"How would I try?" she countered.

She watched him look at her lips and involuntarily lick his own. That was the cruncher for Rosalie. Within a second she had jumped up from where she sat and aimed her lips for his. When they connected with a heavy impact, both of them lost all their senses. She climbed onto his lap, savagely groping his shirt, trying to feel his muscles underneath. Matthew slid his hands under her shirt. When skin touched skin it was as if a massive electric shock passed between them. The air was thick with desire and the desperation to touch each other. Rosalie sat astride him, feeling his need for her and squeezing him with her thighs. She felt Matthew suck in a breath of excitement, which only spurred her on to get his shirt out of the way. In the end she ripped it from

Nothing ventured, nothing gained

his body, sending buttons flying and reflecting off the walls. They vaguely noticed the ripping of the shirt and the buttons, as they were too wrapped up in the moment and in each other to notice anything or anyone else around them. Matthew gathered her hair in his hands and bunched it up as he opened her mouth wider to receive his tongue, to kiss her more deeply. He wanted to taste all of her; he wanted to taste her *everywhere*. He dropped her hair and pulled her shirt over her head, so he could look at her breasts spilling over her black bra. He unclipped it and her breasts tumbled free. He put his hands underneath them, weighing them as he looked at Rosalie's head while it fell back. He lightly slid his thumb across her hard nipples and she groaned. He smiled brightly at her, amazed that this was actually happening. After dreaming about it long enough, after hoping that he would hear her groan with pleasure that he had caused, it was all happening. Suddenly, Rosalie's head snapped forward and she looked him directly in the eye. He applied pressure to her nipple and she bit her lip. He knew she was trying to hold back, because she was trying not to be the first one who gave into her enjoyment. He bent his head to her hardened nipple and pulled it gently between his teeth. His tongue lightly swept across it, which made her bite her lip harder, and then finally he pulled it into his mouth and began to suck it as his thumb massaged the other one. Rosalie shook her head from side to side until she finally gave into her desires and pushed Matthew's head closer to her breast as she tugged at his hair.

After his teasing, he released her nipple and pulled her lips back down to his. Rosalie responded by biting his lower lip, then running her own tongue around his mouth before kissing him deeply. She ran her hands over his chest and felt hard, toned muscles. Then she trailed her fingertips down each muscle, feather-light touches which drove Matthew crazy. He was the first to cave in this time as he roughly pulled her down so she lay on top of him, and then he rolled over, crushing her under him, onto the floor, until he looked down into her face. She smiled mischievously as she pulled his jeans down over his hips and legs. Then she lifted her fingers into the waistband of his boxers, where she gently slid her fingers inside until she hit on what she wanted to find. The boxers were soon discarded and muscle cords stood out in Matthew's neck as he raised it higher, showing his utter bliss. She pushed and prodded with her fingers, pulling his foreskin slightly away from his body, which earned a deep groan from the depths of Matthew's throat.

"Jesus, Brown eyes," he gasped, his face a mask of fulfilment and concentration. His eyes were firmly closed as he raised himself higher so they both looked down and saw his penis standing tall and strong. He looked at Rosalie and basked in the fascination which was showing in her face. Then her eyes met his and it was as if a silent message had been sent between them. Let's do this together. Let's be there in the moment.

Nothing ventured, nothing gained

She pulled her trousers off with impatience and as she went to pull her knickers down, he shook his head and lifted his hand to do it himself. His hand looked so big on her brown skin as he hooked one finger under the outline of her frilly knickers and pulled them down, slowly, leisurely, as if he had all the time in the world to watch her. His eyes hungrily ate up the sight of her, and trailed lower and lower until her knickers were free of her body. He held them up and threw them across the room. He then pressed his lower half to hers, making her feel the size of his need, then to tease her he placed his penis just around the centre of her universe. She opened her thighs wider for his body to fit and he gently kissed her on the mouth. She could feel him position himself, and the sudden rush of desire, of her urgent need, engulfed her to a point where she could see no return. He penetrated her gently, and she gasped with the sheer thrill of how right he felt. He moved slowly at first, careful to make sure Rosalie was OK, but his need soon grew too urgent to ignore. He increased his speed, thrusting harder and harder into her. She met his downward thrusts with her own upward ones. He pushed into her deeper than before, then slowly pulled back, where he lingered for just a minute, then slammed into her with such ferocity that she screamed out. The violence of his passion overtook him as he plunged repeatedly into her, each time more brutal than before.
"Is this what you want?" he demanded, grinding his teeth.

"Just shut up and fuck me!" she cried.

Rosalie lifted her legs even higher until they were wrapped around his midriff, urging him to push deeper, to penetrate her to the fullest. Which he did, as he stifled her screams with short kisses. She arched her spine higher as she felt the first contractions of an orgasm erupting. He felt her tightened around him, felt her inside muscles grip his own, and he cried out in the pure ecstasy of the feeling that was beginning to explode.

"Don't come, don't come," she choked.

"I can't help it," he growled, then he rolled over onto his back lifting her on top of him, where she rode him to the edge, to the highest cliff before he felt himself beginning to fall.

"Shit!" he gasped as he felt the tiny explosions of his orgasm. He rolled over again, covering her small body with the full length of his as he continued to drive himself into her.

"I'm coming....," Rosalie cried again. She felt the intensity of her pleasure explode within her and she knew Matthew felt it too as he groaned in despair. But still he continued plunging inside her moistness, bringing her to yet another extreme sensation. He ruthlessly pushed his hips deeper into her, as he felt the shuddering spasms begin to detonate within him, and with a tumultuous groan of torture he felt himself begin to surge his seed into her. His head bowed forward into her neck as he waited for the feeling to pass. They both breathed heavily, the air hot and sticky, their bodies slick with sweat. A while later, he lifted his head from her neck and smiled lazily down at her.

Nothing ventured, nothing gained

His eyes looked dazed, as if his pupils had melted into his iris. He looked so relaxed that she had trouble thinking it was actually the Matthew Mason she knew. She hadn't imagined that he would be that good at sex. If she had known she would have jumped into the sack with him a lot earlier. He rolled over onto his back next to her and linked his fingers between hers. He brought their hands up to his mouth and kissed them.

"That was probably the best time I have ever had," Rosalie smiled dreamily as she recalled those moments of such pleasure she thought she would die if she didn't have any release.

Matthew opened his arm up for her to snuggle into. She fitted perfectly and he could just imagine them being like this in their own house, when they eventually moved in with each other. Which he had no doubt that they would. He was happy thinking about their future when they heard keys turning in the door.

"FUCK!" shouted Rosalie as she jumped up from Matthew and searched for her clothes frantically. Matthew jumped up too, looking for his shirt. When he found it ripped he looked to Rosalie to ask what had happened; he felt his heart stutter because that's when he really saw her. Saw her, naked, searching for her clothes. Her body was curvy and precious, and he felt such a surge of love burst through his chest, he found it hard to breathe.

"Neus. Do not come in," she shouted to the door as she picked up Matthew's trousers and threw them at him. He just stood there, looking at her.

"Yeah, yeah. I'm not interested if you guys screwed or not, goodnight," Neus shouted, followed by footsteps going up the stairs.

Rosalie let out a sigh of relief as she turned to see Matthew just staring at her.

"What?" she asked, suddenly self-conscious at her state of nakedness.

"You're beautiful," he said. She gave him a small smile and then turned around to pick up her jeans.

"Tell me something," she said as she pulled them on, her back still to Matthew.

"What?"

"Do you have sex with all women like that or is it just me?" She didn't know why she had to bring this up now, but she didn't feel right about not doing so. She had to face the truth that she didn't know anything about Matthew, only that he was a kind man and a good lover. Yes, some would say that was enough, but not for her. She needed to know about his family, his past, and why it was so important to him that Robin be looked after. She also wanted to get straight about these models that he had made jokes about.

"I don't understand," Matthew replied, looking at her back.

"I was just wondering if I'm a notch on your bedpost or if I am something…different." She winced at her choice of words and mentally slapped herself for bringing this up now, especially after they'd both experienced something special. But that was the point, she told herself, was it special? Or was it just another regular sex encounter for him?

Nothing ventured, nothing gained

"Is that a normal night of sex or was that an extra burst of energy?"
"Brown eyes, don't do this now." He sighed. "Don't ruin what took place here tonight."
"I'm not ruining anything," she said, turning towards him. "I'm just trying to make sense of what happened tonight. That's all."
"It's…..you know it was special."
"Yes, to me it was special. But to you?"
"It was….special as well. Look," he said more firmly. "Stop it."
"Scared of what you have to lie about?"
Matthew's mouth opened wide in shock. "How dare you," he uttered, but Rosalie cut him off.
"I know nothing about you. You tell me nothing! How can I know if what I feel is real if I don't know if it's an everyday occurrence to you?"
"Brown eyes…"
"No! You can't call me that! Look, you may think I'm just an emotional woman, which yeah I am, but I need to know!"
"You've got to know," he repeated.
"Yes! I've got to know if my love for you is…." She stopped talking, realizing she'd just said the L word. Matthew seemed to have noticed it as well, because he'd stopped breathing.
"Uh…I mean….I didn't mean what…."
Matthew's mobile started ringing and he fumbled to find it.
"Yeah?" he breathed into it. Rosalie turned away, not wanting him to see the tears in her eyes, nor the disappointment in the fact that he hadn't said it back.

"I'll be right there," he said and closed the phone. "Look, Rosalie, I'll phone you. I'm sorry it's an emergency and I can't…"

"Just go" she interrupted. She heard him gather his things and walk towards the door. He turned back towards her, intending to give her a kiss, but when she gave him her cheek he sighed and said, "I will phone you as soon as I can." All she could do was nod mutely, and then when she heard him leave, she cried. Hot, thick and fast tears, until Neus came down and comforted her. She wouldn't admit to Neus that she was also crying for the fact that he was right, Matthew had got a phone call and he had left. Only he had got what he wanted beforehand.

Nothing ventured, nothing gained

Chapter twelve

Rosalie sat at her computer, her hands hovering over the keyboard, mentally spelling out what she was about to type. She needed to know, she needed to understand, so why did she feel so guilty? She wasn't one to read gossip magazines or take much notice of the tabloids, so of course she wouldn't know anything about him. Well, she wouldn't know anything *true* about him. Not that typing his name into the internet would be any better, she reminded herself, but this way it didn't feel so much of a betrayal. It had been three days since she had slept with him, and he'd tried calling her at least five times a day. Perhaps, she mused, that should tell me how he feels. But Rosalie had dodged all his calls, even his visits up to Acorn stables, where Lesley had covered for her.

Rosalie knew she wasn't dodging him just because she could, but she couldn't shake the uneasy feeling she'd had when she had admitted to loving him, and getting the feeling that that was the last thing he wanted. It was something in his eyes, Rosalie had decided, that gave him away. (Rosalie also didn't like to admit that her pride had been stung a little when he hadn't said that he loved her too.) Then, after a day or so of crying and cursing Matthew, she had begun to think about it logically. Why would he not want someone to love him? Then when Gwen had confessed about knowing Matthew was married, or ex-married, as Gwen had put it, she knew there was more to this than the typical man-scared-ofcommitment case.

Rosalie needed to get her head around a concept like Matthew. He was mysterious and unpredictable. He had two sides to him, but she knew one of them was just an act. Underneath his arrogant and cheeky exterior, Rosalie had found that there were many more layers to him, all of which perhaps she'd never uncover, but she wasn't going to give up on him, as so many others had appeared to do. The only reason she wasn't speaking to him was because she felt guilty. Guilty about going behind his back to find out about him. She didn't like it, but she thought it would help to have the full view from everyone and then go to him and see what he told her. She had also noticed that Robin had been on edge these past few days as well. After Gwen telling her about what Robin had said, Robin hadn't really spoken to anyone. That was fine with Rosalie, because for some reason, if Robin did speak to her it would make her feel even guiltier. She typed in Matthew Mason and waited for the results to come up. She guessed most results would just come up with the stars that he represented, but there might be background knowledge on him somewhere among the twenty thousand results. Rosalie groaned, twenty thousand was too many; she wouldn't go through all of them. Two hours later, Neus was fast asleep as well as Robin. Rosalie stared tiredly at the computer screen and clicked on the next result.

MASON SCORES CONTRACT FOR BOOP!

She sighed. She was bored of this now.

Nothing ventured, nothing gained

"I should have gone straight to him," she muttered as she opened one more result.
She quickly glanced down the newspaper column from an Irish newspaper in Dublin.
LUKE MASON COMMITS SUICIDE!
The headline jumped out at Rosalie as her eyes grew wide and her mind started spinning. Luke Mason? Matthew had never mentioned a Luke. Then she snorted: Matthew had never mentioned any of his family.
"Luke Mason, aged twenty seven, committed suicide last night while inside Mountjoy Prison, situated in Dublin," Rosalie read allowed, squinting her eyes against the screen to see well. It was a small amount of information, about six or seven lines, but held so many answers to her questions that Rosalie had to read on.
"Government officials are saying that it he was found in the early hours of this morning in his cell, which he had up to the previous night been sharing with another inmate. Luke Mason was serving a life sentence for the well-known murder of Carmen Mason, his sister-in-law. There is no comment from Luke Mason's family at this time."
Rosalie's eyes flew back to the sister-in-law line. Carmen Mason? Then everything came to her in such a rush of pressure that she tore her eyes away from the screen and rubbed her temples. She got up on weak legs and went down the hallway to the kitchen. If Carmen was Luke's sister in law and Matthew had been married……the concept was too much for her to think about. So instead, she opened the fridge and pulled out a

bottle of wine. She almost wished she hadn't seen those seven lines now, because instead of answering her questions, all it did was create more.

Matthew paced impatiently up and down his office. His hand was pressed thoughtfully to his chin as he considered his options. Tili had just come in to give him news on the new contract he had scored for Sandy Shine, saying that the newspapers didn't agree with the exclusive interview he had set up for her with *Real Life!* And now *Booty!* was complaining that he had verbally said that they had the interview in the bag. Yes, perhaps he may have mentioned it a few months ago, but his mind was so preoccupied at the moment that he couldn't remember half the things he'd said. Of course, with the exception of four days ago after he and Rosalie had slept with each other. Oh yes, he remembered every detail about that conversation. But, as Tili and his mother pointed out, his mind wasn't focused on his work, which was in dire need of some attention. Matthew was annoyed with letting himself lose control. All over a woman! It had happened this way before. First he would become besotted, wouldn't listen to any advice given to him, would fall head over heels in love with her, then he was screwed over and the pain was unbearable. When Rosalie had said she loved him, it was if a barrier had put itself up within him, not allowing her words to reach him, not allowing himself to get hurt again. Which is why now, he was able to concentrate on his work.

Nothing ventured, nothing gained

Yes, he had been calling her, but he was ashamed to admit that even though he'd called her so many times, he had been restraining himself from calling more frequently. OK, he conceded, perhaps she wasn't as out of his thoughts as he wished.

"Tili!" he shouted towards his open door.

"Yes, Mr Mason?" she asked, coming to stand at the doorway.

"Get our mole on the phone, tell him to pass the word around that the interview will go to the highest bidder, and this time it will be exclusive at the price."

"Our mole?" she asked, trying to place the man Matthew was talking about.

"David," he said, referring to his inside, right-hand man, who knew everything that was going on, what deals and what new hot opportunities were appearing.

"OK. Anything else?"

"No, I'll call you in a sec when I find a solution to the Boop dilemma."

"OK. Oh, and your mother said she wanted to speak to you later on."

Matthew sighed. No doubt his mother would be spinning more I-won't-be-here-for-ever conversations his way. He didn't like to admit they unsettled him. Yes, he knew that everyone died and it was something no one could buy or lie themselves out of, but he didn't like to think about it too much. After all, life was already pressurising and sometimes sad without the added fear of death hanging over your head all the time.

Perhaps he could pray to God, maybe He'd do something to help his mother through whatever emotions she was experiencing at this time. Yes, He would certainly help, as He had helped in the past. Matthew snorted to himself; he was becoming too sarcastic for his own good in his old age. Truth was, even though he was only thirty, compared to most it was an old age to be. He felt older than his years most of the time; his job stole his energy and brain space. He only felt relaxed when….Matthew laughed without any humour in it. Of course, the irony of the situation entered his mind. The woman who caused him so much pain and distraction was the only woman who could take away the pain and make him feel happy.

"Oh, so you've done the turn. Well done," Jack said to his wife.
"Yes," she answered excitedly, either ignoring or not noticing Jack's sardonic expression.
Mary turned to Rosalie who was standing proudly next to Merlin, patting his back.
In two days the horse show would be here and Rosalie knew Mary was feeling the butterflies already.
"Well, let's just hope you do it right when it matters," Jack said, smiling slickly as his eyes twinkled at Rosalie. She mentally pretended to be sick.
"Oh, she will," Rosalie assured him.
"Well, I hope I will." Mary corrected Rosalie, looking at her with shy eyes. Even though Mary wasn't really her type of person, she couldn't help

Nothing ventured, nothing gained

but hope she would do well and prove to everyone she could do it.

"Well, come on Merlin, let's get you to the field," Mary said, pulling gently on the reins and with a few seconds of hesitation Merlin stepped slowly forward, clearly too lazy to put much effort into it.

"Sucker, come here!" Rosalie shouted as she ran in and out between Merlin's legs. But Rosalie had to laugh when the only reaction Sucker provoked was a glance in her direction and a sigh from Merlin's nose. Rosalie imagined Merlin raising his eyebrow as if to say, what are you doing?

She bent to pick Sucker up, then turned around and bumped into Jack. She was startled because she'd assumed he'd gone, but he hadn't and now she knew that another sinner/saint conversation was going to take place.

"So, are you still seeing that guy?" Rosalie hoped the pain hadn't shown in her eyes at the mention of Matthew. She was still unsure how to approach him about what she'd discovered. She hadn't received a call from him recently and was scared that he was going off her.

"Yes," she replied shortly as she walked off.

"So, does he make you come?"

Rosalie swung around, nearly hitting Jack in the face with her elbow. She was disappointed she hadn't. Her mouth opened and closed, shocked at the bold and irrational question. Then she gave a laugh of disbelief.

He looked confused at her laugh, but nevertheless laughed along with her.

"It's none of your business, Jack, and to be

honest, I can't believe I ever thought of you as…well, anything else other than a condescending, fake, self-loving, arrogant prick!"

He looked down at his hands then back at her. He scratched his cheek, unsure of what to say.

"Well, does he?" he eventually asked.

"Yes. Like a freight train, so hard and so fast that I have never felt anything like it before."

Jack was quiet and Rosalie laughed again. "Happy now? Was that what you wanted to know?"

"Nah, I was just wanting to find out if you were satisfied, 'cos," he leant in further, "I can always do that job if you want" and he gave a wag of his eyebrows.

She shook her head. "Just bugger off and go to your wife. She's a great woman."

"Yeah, but not great in the bed department."

"Then why marry her if you were planning to stray anyway?"

Jack shrugged, uncomfortable with the seriousness this conversation had caused.

"Why do men do that?" she asked, almost to herself. "Lead a woman on, thinking everything is hunkydory, but behind their backs just screw whatever moves, but still go home for tea."

"And what about the women who have sex with these men, knowing full well that they belong to another, or will be soon, but still do it, not caring who they hurt or how much." Rosalie sighed and stroked Sucker. "Women like me."

Jack shifted backwards, towards an exit, wanting to escape this conversation.

Nothing ventured, nothing gained

Rosalie looked up at him, as if remembering he was there. With one look at his face she shook her head. "You can't deal with it, can you? Someone's emotions?"
"I can, but look Lee, you're not my problem any more."
"Then why don't you go away? Like I said you should do all those months ago?"
"I'm going. Christ, that guy of your needs to seriously to give you one."
That was enough for Rosalie. She put Sucker down, anger displaying on her pretty face, and marched towards Jack, who instantly backed away.
"You bastard!" she cursed as she broke in a run after him. He ran down the track, past the machinery and tripped over a tree root sticking out of the ground. Rosalie stopped running and stood watching him ten feet back. He was scrambling on the ground looking for his green contact lens that had fallen out. When he looked at her, she burst out laughing, for one eye was blue and the other green. He frowned at her and narrowed his different-coloured eyes as she doubled over. Narrowing them and squinting at her made it worse!
"Please have mercy! I can't take any more stomach cramps from laughing," she gasped, bursting out in a fresh bout of laughter as he stomped past, looking like a big kid.
She smiled sadly to herself, thinking about her past mistakes as she looked at one walking away. She couldn't shake the feeling that if Matthew ever

found out about Jack, he would lose all respect for her. Because, on what she had assumed and what Gwen had told her, Carmen might have betrayed him in some way while they were married. Hadn't she and Jack done the same thing to Mary?

"Hold on," Matthew said, rubbing his eyes as he leant forward, propping his elbows up on the desk. "So you're telling me that she knows I was married?" he asked again, to be absolutely clear. Beth nodded gravely and looked at her son. She knew she should have told him sooner, but she had been too worried about breaking the news of her health to him. So now, she was telling him about Rose, then afterwards, she'd tell him about her.
"So she knows about Carmen?"
"She knows it ended. But not how and not why."
Matthew nodded absently. "I guess it's a miracle that she hadn't found out about it sooner."
"Why, son?"
He looked at his mother. "I'm always in the press; something might have come up about me."
"No," Beth said firmly. "When we left Ireland, we left it there, it didn't follow us."
"Mum, everything follows us. It's haunting us now and probably will ruin my chance with Rosalie."
"Well, at least you're admitting that you want to have a chance with her," Beth said, trying to make light of the conversation.
He narrowed his eyes. "Yes. Thank God you came clean about trying to set us up though, otherwise

Nothing ventured, nothing gained

I'd be none the wiser at what she knew."
"I just felt you should know," Beth explained, placing her hand on his arm.
He sighed and took her hand. "Mum, I don't know what do now."
"Well, you go to see her of course."
"But God knows what she thinks happened with Carmen, what if she doesn't want to see me?"
"That's not Mason talk. You don't run away, you go and give her your story. The *real* story."
"She might not want to hear it."
"Make her hear it."
Matthew sighed and ran a hand thorough his ink-black hair. "Right, OK, I will. I'll go now."
Matthew got up and went to the door, but then turned when his mother called him back.
"Before you go," Beth took a deep breath, "there's something you need to know…."

"Oh God," Rosalie said, her face pinching with concern for Matthew. Gwen sat opposite her, after breaking the news that Beth Mason had breast cancer.
"They can do things though," Rosalie started before Gwen put her hand up.
"Beth told me to tell you because Matthew needs help. He was terribly upset, started crying, throwing things." Gwen looked Rosalie directly in the eye. "He needs you. And Beth wanted me to tell you that."
"Yes, I'll go right over now," she said as she got up and put Sucker on Gwen's lap. Before Gwen had the chance to tell her to be careful, Rosalie had

already gone.

"What's that all about?" Neus asked, coming into the kitchen.

Gwen smiled and looked at him. "Rose is just going to be with Matthew tonight. I hope they have a spare toothbrush."

Neus frowned, unsure why Gwen had said that, but then shrugged.

"How's Tili?" she asked casually.

"Don't know. I haven't seen her since last week."

"Anything happen?" Gwen enquired, getting up and pouring herself a cup of tea.

Neus flopped down at the kitchen table. "Well….yes and no."

"Tell me."

"How come you want to know?"

"OK," Gwen said, putting down her cup as she sat down. "I'll come clean with you. I and Beth Mason, Matthew's mother, have been trying to set Rose and him up. And then we got a bit excited that it was working and we tried to set you and Tili up as well."

"But I asked her out."

"Yes, but why do you think she was at bingo in the first place?"

Neus thought for a second, and then as everything seemed to make sense he started to grin. Gwen was glad, because she couldn't stand it if he were angry with her.

"My my, Gwen, we certainly didn't see you coming, did we?"

Gwen smiled mysteriously then laughed as Neus rolled his eyes.

Nothing ventured, nothing gained

"Well, I guess it worked with Matthew and Lee, but then again, I think it would have worked without you interfering."
"Yes. But it needed a little push."
"More than a push, more like a kick up the arse to get those two into gear!"
"Language. And anyway, I truly believe that they are right for each other."
"I guess. But not me and Tili."
"Why ever not?"
"Do you want a lie or the real thing?"
"The real thing please."
"Well, we were about to have sex, and then she started checking me out for sexually transmitted disease. Like genital warts and stuff. It was like a cold bucket of water had been poured into my lap."
Gwen was quiet for a while then laughed. "I said the truth, Neus!" She got up and went to make some sandwiches.
Neus just grinned widely.
"You know, Gwen, I don't know if I and Rosalie could survive without you," he said, getting up and kissing her on the cheek.
Gwen blushed and patted her hair in place. "You two would be fine without me."
"No, we wouldn't. And let's hope we never find out."
Gwen watched Neus take a bottle of beer out of the fridge. Gwen knew she wouldn't change anything about her life. It was times like these when it was good to look around and see what you really had. And Gwen knew what she had was

special.

The hard droplets of rain hit the windscreen thick and fast. Rosalie increased Ed's wipers and accelerated down Reading Road, forgetting to stop at the zebra crossing. She went fast past the fish and chip shop and petrol stations without taking much of her surroundings in. All she could think of was getting to Matthew. She couldn't imagine what he must be feeling, and after finding out about his mother, nothing but heartbroken was in her mind. At this moment in time, Rosalie couldn't have cared less if Matthew had killed Carmen or if Luke had killed Carmen or even Matthew's dad had killed her, all she cared about was seeing Matthew. All she wanted to do was hold him, rock him back and forth, tell him it was OK, and be there for him. That was what love meant at the end of the day, being there for each other regardless of the situation. She vaguely heard the horn of another car telling her to move over, which she did, rather dramatically and nearly knocking the mirror off a parked car. She drove up Duke Street, past the crowded Wimpy with teenagers running inside trying to get out of the rain, past the town centre, which was now deserted and dripping wet, and down Bell Street. She wouldn't ask about Carmen, Luke or his family tonight, it didn't matter to her any more. She loved Matthew with all her heart and couldn't stand him feeling sadness and despair without her there to help him through it.
Of course, she knew about Gwen's association

Nothing ventured, nothing gained

with Beth now, it all made sense. How she and Matthew had been at the same restaurant, how convenient it was that Gwen already had plans when Matthew came over.

She flew past the camp site and the gardening centre as she made her way into Hambledon. It was still raining but it had lightened up a little. About five minutes later she was pulling into the Maybrew Mansion, past the long winding tracks, surrounded by trees and bushes, all finely cut, and down the gravel towards the entrance. She was thankful the gate wasn't closed as she drove past it and pulled up beside the angel fountain that stood in the middle of the drive, creating a circle of grass and flowers around it. Rosalie got out of Ed, leaving him unlocked as she didn't imagine that anyone would steal him.

She knocked on the double doors, waited a few minutes, and then the door was opened and she assumed Beth Mason was standing in front of her.

"Rose," she said warmly, opening the door wider, allowing her to enter. The sight took Rosalie's breath away, as she'd only seen the grounds of Maybrew Mansion before. But they didn't do justice to the building itself. Her eyes widened as she looked up and saw a sparkling chandelier hanging from the top, in the centre of the white carved ceiling.

Rosalie quickly snapped herself back to the present. She wanted to look around, but the need to see Matthew was so great that she had to go to him.

Beth must have read her expression as she

smiled and said, "We'll look later. Now, Matthew's upstairs in his office. Tili isn't there any more."

Rosalie nodded, not sure what to say. Should she offer her sympathy? Or just keep quiet?

"He doesn't know you're here, but I think he'd really appreciate it."

"Um…" Rosalie began, but Beth shook her head and smiled again.

"We'll talk later, go and see him."

"Thanks," she said as she turned towards the stairs. Rosalie ran up the right-hand staircase as she looked towards the left, and marvelled at how they met in the middle. But she would marvel more later on, right now it was Matthew she needed to think about.

She walked along a corridor and saw a slice of light peep its way through the crack of a closed door. She assumed this was Matthew's office, and without knocking she walked in. He was sitting at his desk, his head bowed in his hands, and she thought he was crying. She took a hesitant step forward, unsure whether he would like to be left alone. But as he looked up to see her standing there, she had no time to think about leaving. It was as if she had fallen asleep and missed something, because the next thing she knew he was in her arms, hugging her tightly, and he was sobbing into her shoulder as she stroked his neck and told him it would be OK.

She kissed his neck and lightly trailed her fingers down his cheek as he lifted his head and looked down at her. His eyes were swollen from crying and his nose bright red. She couldn't help but

Nothing ventured, nothing gained

smile when he self-consciously wrinkled it.
"Oh, Matthew," she sighed, looking into his eyes and feeling her heart melt. He looked so much like a lost boy, so vulnerable and young, even innocent, she decided. He lifted his hand and cupped her cheek; she turned her head and kissed his palm.
"Brown eyes," he whispered as she looked up at him again. "Where do I start?" he said, resting his forehead against hers.
"Shh," she replied, pressing her lips gently to his. "It doesn't matter. We'll talk later." As she spoke, her lips brushed his gently. "We're just here together for now."
They held each other a while, just standing with their arms wrapped around their bodies, relaxing in their own company.
Eventually, Matthew lifted his head and smiled as Rosalie's eyes opened wearily.
"Hmm. I feel so relaxed," she whispered, then laughed as she swayed a little. Matthew straightened her and kissed her gently.
"I suppose we'd better talk."
"We don't have to. Whatever you want to do, Matt."
"I do want to talk. We need to get thing straight between us, and...." He ran a hand through his hair. "I guess you know about my mother."
She nodded. "Gwen told me."
He smiled weakly. "A bit of a trick they were up to, huh?"
"Yeah. Well, now I know never to let appearances deceive me."

He took her hand and led her to the desk, where he sat her down in his chair and he sat on the desk, his legs dangling over the side. Rosalie smiled, because seeing Matthew sitting on the desk was another sight she hadn't thought she would see.

"Where shall we start?" he asked.

"Um....your mother?"

"Yeah. My mother." Matthew was silent for a minute or two, then he looked into Rosalie's eyes, took her hand and held it between his own.

"She's got breast cancer. She found out a month ago, but didn't want to tell me because, well," he shrugged, "she didn't think I would need the extra hassle."

Rosalie's eyebrows rose and he laughed, but humourlessly. "Her words, not mine."

"But surely she knows that you wouldn't have cared about what time she told you?"

"That's what I said, but she said that she knew what strains this job causes me and what with Kevin and Robin....she said it wasn't the right time. "So I shouted at her, and said it was never going to be the right time to tell me she was dying."

"She won't die," Rosalie said.

Matthew shook his head and gave a sigh. "I don't know anything any more."

"Surely they can operate? Make her better..."

"Yes, they will, she's going to the hospital in two days, but...it's the risk of it coming back. God! I shouted at her having cancer. How low can I go?"

"You were upset, Beth knows that."

Nothing ventured, nothing gained

"No, it doesn't make it right. I should be strong for her. She's always been strong for me when it came to Carmen…"
They were both silent.
"I can't believe she didn't tell me sooner," Matthew said. "I must have neglected her that much and been so distant from her, that she would keep something like this to herself all this time." Matthew fiddled with Rosalie's fingers as he spoke. "She's been so strong for all of us, and when the time came for her to rest and me to be strong, I let her down."
"You couldn't have done anything if you didn't know," Rosalie pointed out.
"I know. But it doesn't make the guilt any easier, does it?"
"No, it doesn't," Rosalie said quietly.
He looked at her and held her hand tighter. "You bring so many emotions to the surface, Brown eyes, I just hope you can understand about me and my past."
"Nothing will make a difference to how I feel about you."
"It will. You'll find out about my family and run a bloody mile," he said as he dropped her hand and went to stand by the window.
"Matt…"
"No!" he suddenly shouted. "Don't use that soft voice on me! I can't stand it. Why, God why have I given my heart to someone else after swearing that I wouldn't?"
"Matthew, please, let's just talk about it."
"Rosalie, you don't know me and don't pretend to."

"Well, if you'd just tell me, then maybe I would know," she replied tightly.

"What? So you can use it as an excuse for not being with me?"

"Christ Almighty! I'm trying to be supportive here and I'm trying to understand, but I can't when you talk in fucking riddles!"

"Riddles are the only thing keeping you here. Looking at me like you love me. But you don't, Brown eyes, you bloody don't," he spat.

"Don't tell me how I feel!" she shouted.

"I've seen it all before. All the lies, the looks, the words I've heard from a woman I thought loved me...then you come along and do the same thing!"

"I haven't done anything! And how dare you just assume what I will do? You really don't know me at all, do you?"

"I know you too well. Which is why I'm scared that you'll go!" he shouted again, looking at her with anger and sadness.

Rosalie took some breaths, willing with herself to calm down. She loved him, she knew she did, and she also knew that whatever he told her wouldn't alter her feelings. She just wished he would see that too.

"Matt, tell me what happened, tell me what's going on in your head. Please," she said when he began to shake his head. "Let me understand."

For a while they stared at each other, until Matthew sighed and pulled her into his arms, crushing her closely to his body, murmuring his apologies over and over again into her ears. He

Nothing ventured, nothing gained

ran his hands through her hair and kissed her forehead.

She looked up and saw him watching her. She stretched her head and kissed him on the mouth. He responded gently, savouring her taste, hoping that this wouldn't be the last kiss they shared. When she pulled back she smiled at him with such tenderness that Matthew could feel his heart tug.

Rosalie took his hand and led him over to the sofa in the corner. She assumed it was for when clients came over, but it also made the daunting office less scary. They sat down together and she kept hold of his hand, waiting for him to explain.

"About fifteen years ago, my parents took in a boy named Luke. He was five years older than me and had destruction on his mind. Of course, I don't even think he knew what destruction he would do in the future. My parents took him in because they so desperately wanted another son. It was a known tradition that in the Mason family there were always at least two boys each generation. I don't know if it was true, but that's what my dad told me when Luke came to stay with us."

"Why did your parents take in someone as old as Luke?" Rosalie asked.

"Well, I guess because my mother couldn't go through the pressure and strain on her body of having another baby. And as for his age, well, I think they thought he was a nice young lad and it would be good if he was there to look after me and the land we had, when my father died. Anyway, him being twenty and me being fifteen, well, you can imagine how we got on. It wasn't pretty. A lot of teasing and a lot of hatred and bitter competition. If I got something, Luke would get something better; if I brought a girlfriend home, he'd bring a prettier one home, or even cop off with mine. The girls always went crazy for Luke. Which, as you can imagine, did nothing for my teenage ego."

Matthew tried a weak smile. "Well, whatever we had going in between us, my parents loved him. They only ever saw the helpful, kind, considerate son they thought he was. They never saw the side of him that I saw. The conniving, cheating, lying side he managed to hide so well.

"When I was nineteen, I met a girl called Carmen O'Connel. She was an Irish girl through and through, and was very loving. I fell in love with her. Hard and fast, painfully and pleasurably, all the emotions you could feel when in love, I felt. I thought she felt them too; she was also acting as if I was the best thing in her life. It wasn't until later on that I found out at that time she was being sweet talked by Luke.

"By twenty I asked her to marry me. My parents objected, saying I was too young, too immature, all those usual things parents say when they want you to stop what you're doing. I didn't listen, me being the strong-headed, stubborn idiot I am, I was convinced she loved me and I knew I loved her more than anything else.

"By twenty-one I was married. Looking back now I don't know why she ever agreed to marry me if she was screwing Luke, but the bitter part of me reckons it was Luke still trying to get one over

Nothing ventured, nothing gained

me."
"How do you mean?" Rosalie wondered.
"Well, me marrying the girl he was screwing and who, at the time, was in love with him was a pretty evil thing to do. He made me to look a fool again, having what he didn't want. Of course, at that time I didn't know any of this. I was none the wiser, so to speak.
I just thought everything was fine and dandy.
"But then, Carmen became ill. She was urinating a lot more than usual, which at the time I didn't think anything of ; I just assumed she'd had a lot to drink. Then she told me that she was having many headaches, that she felt tired all the time. I offered to take her to a doctor, but she said no, she didn't want to go.
"She eventually did when she started experiencing a fever, and when I saw that her glands had swollen up in her neck, I knew something was definitely wrong.
"It was then she was tested, they found she had a sexually transmitted disease. I obviously was confused because I knew I hadn't had it, then after the initial effect of the news wore off it was clear that she had been cheating on me."
"What did she have?" Rosalie asked, squeezing his hand encouragingly
"At that point it was gonorrhoea. But it was only later, after more tests, that they found she was HIV positive. Apparently if you have a sexually transmitted disease already, then you're more prone to getting HIV while having sex with a guy who already has it.

So, I asked her who she'd been sleeping with, did he know that he had this disease and did he know he'd given it to her. I will always remember her answer. She said, 'He wouldn't know, he loves me.'"

Matthew bowed his head and Rosalie reached out to touch him. She was saddened to see him flinch. He lifted his head and look at her. Then he sighed again as he held up her hand to his cheek.

"I couldn't get my head around it; really, I just couldn't believe it. I always thought, me being young and in love, that she loved me and was faithful. I also, for some reason, thought that HIV and Aids only occurred in homosexual men. I mean, Freddy Mercury for example, I don't know why I thought that, but God; I was so young and foolish. After I got myself checked out and the results were negative, I didn't know what to do.

"So, like the idiot I was, I just pretended it wasn't happening. That she hadn't cheated on me and that she was just sick. At that point I was twenty-one and Luke was twenty-six."

Rosalie thought back to the age when Luke had died and she recalled it had been twenty-seven.

"It all came to a head the day I found out it was Luke who had infected Carmen, and who had the disease himself. She told me on a Saturday morning, as she lay in her bed, feeling sick and tired, she just calmly said, 'Your brother did this to me and I want you to know.' I'm not sure what made her tell me, I believe she felt as if she had suffered enough.

"Well, I marched right over to my parent's house –

Nothing ventured, nothing gained

at that point me and Carmen lived in a small cottage on the land – and went to find Luke. My father followed me, obviously worried at what I'd do. I assumed he didn't know about any of this and I don't think he did, but he knew something was wrong.
"There I confronted Luke, and the fucking bastard wasn't even sorry. He said that he had given her a disease but it wasn't HIV because he knew he didn't have that. He started playing with my head, telling me that she was too good for me anyway and that she had every right to go looking somewhere else for a bit of decent loving.
"When I think back now, I feel sorry for my father. Listening to his golden boy admit to screwing his sister-in-law and showing his true colours. Poor dad, he didn't have a clue about any of it. So, Luke carried on tormenting me, making me angry, making me want to kill him for betraying me and hurting Carmen, because regardless of the fact that she had cheated on me, I still loved her. Crazy, isn't it? I should have hated her, and I did in a way, but I still loved her."
"I ended up punching Luke in the face. It wasn't half of what I wanted to do to him, but Dad had pulled me back and shouted at me to go home and that he'd deal with Luke. So I went and for a while things remained as they were. Me lying to myself, Carmen dealing with her own problems, and I never saw Luke."
"Until one day I was coming home and saw Luke and Carmen arguing in the kitchen. For a moment I just watched, seeing how they shouted at one

another, how their faces changed with each expression. It was then I left. I didn't go in. I knew there was no point; they'd still do whatever the hell they wanted to do because that's what they were like. Selfish."

"It was the next morning that I and my parents got news of Carmen's death and Luke's arrest. It was so much to take in at once that I was numb. Nothing seemed real; I mean, this was stuff that happened in books and films, not in real life, right?"

"But it was all true. All of it. The witnesses saying they saw Luke handling her dead body, his fingerprints all over her body, his blood, presumably where she'd hit him, on her clothes. That was how the courts decided it wasn't planned, because if it was, who would be so careless as to leave those type of trails around? It was argued that Luke was temporarily insane, making him kill her out of anger. I guess meaning he didn't know what he was doing."

"It was about a year after her murder and Luke serving a life sentence that he killed himself. He wrote a letter to all of us, saying he didn't deserve a life, even a life in prison."

"To me, he was a bloody coward for killing himself; he couldn't live up to what he'd done so he took the easy way out."

"My mother and father were upset, even after everything, and I guess I was: not for him, but for all the possibilities that could have happened, if he'd just allowed it. I still don't know to this day if he had given Carmen HIV, I never really found out

Nothing ventured, nothing gained

because that wasn't the point. He killed her in the heat of their argument and I've lived with the guilt of walking away from her that night. Because if I hadn't...."

"She still wouldn't be here, Matt," Rosalie said gently.

Matthew looked at her. "I know," he replied quietly "But I could have done something. As for Luke, well, I doubt anyone could have done anything for him, he was hell bent on destroying himself and others around him from the beginning."

"Jesus, you've been through all that? Why aren't you...uh, a nervous wreck?" She laughed at her choice of words.

Matthew smiled. "A lot of time has passed. It's all ancient history now, it's not a part of my life. Of course I still think about them, they never leave my thoughts really, but my bitterness and anger left me a while ago and all I feel now is sadness when I think back. More for Carmen than Luke, I admit. She was just a young woman who was in love with Luke. She didn't really do anything wrong."

"She cheated on you!"

"Compared to what she got in return for that mistake, it doesn't really mean much, does it?"

"No, I don't suppose it does." As they were both quiet in their own thoughts, Rosalie suddenly smacked her forehead and swore.

"What?" Matthew asked.

"I'm just remembering that once I told you I don't condone suicide!"

Matthew laughed.

"No, it's not funny, what did you think of me?" she asked.
"If you think back, you'd recall me agreeing."
"Well, I only said those things to challenge you."
"Challenge me?"
"Yeah, well you turned up looking so self-assured and I wanted to ruffle your composure."
Matthew just laughed at her silliness.
"Well, come on, finish the story. So after Luke died, you and your family left?"
"Yes, we all left because the scandal and the talk were too much for my mother to take. She'd been through a lot and I was more than happy to leave. So we left and came to England."
"That's a far way to go," Rosalie commented as she placed a hand on his knee.
"Well," he said, moving closer to her and pulling her into his arms, "we wanted a complete fresh start. So we came to Henley, one of my Dad's friends had family in Reading and they recommended this town. He was the only friend my father had left, so my dad didn't mind about leaving either."
"So we left, and we lived here at Maybrew, until I decided to get into the PR business and the place to be was London if I wanted to make a go of it. I hooked up with a few guys in the business and...the rest is history."
"So, in the end everything turned out OK?"
"I guess so."
"A happy ending?" she asked smiling, lifting her head to look in his eyes. "Like a fairytale?"
Matthew laughed and smiled more widely. "Well,

Nothing ventured, nothing gained

that depends on whether I become insane."
"Why would you become insane?"
"Well, there's a woman with brown eyes and she seems to recreate all these feelings of insecurity, love and happiness and pain, but you see, I'm scared that I'm kidding myself again into thinking that she loves me back." He peered deeply into her eyes. "Am I kidding myself?"
Rosalie looked into his eyes and smiled brightly. "No. You're not kidding yourself at all."
"So," he said lightly, tracing a finger around the outline of her mouth. "Do you want a tour?"
Rosalie did, knowing the tour would end up in the bedroom, where she so desperately wanted to go, but first, she had to get something off her chest.
She sat up. Immediately seeing the panic in his eyes, she smiled to reassure him.
"There's something you should know."
"OK."
"You know the guy called Jack. Well, I was seeing him up until about two months ago. He's such a vain guy that I can't believe I actually had sex with him. Sorry to be crude, but it was the biggest mistake ever and he's been trying it on ever since I broke it off."
"OK, that's not so bad."
"But the thing is, while I was seeing him, he was seeing someone else, called Mary. And they were engaged." She grimaced as she said it, awaiting Matthew's response.
She looked at him and saw him looking back at her.
"I know it was wrong and stupid of me, which is

why I didn't like myself back then. But, I changed, before I met you."

"You're not still seeing him?"

"God no! He's such a prat and a prick and I hate him and I hate myself for what I did to Mary, who actually is a nice girl."

"I can't put a judgement on you, Brown eyes, I've been an idiot myself. Put it this way." He suddenly smiled as he brought her closer to him. "It doesn't make me love you any less. But it does make me insanely jealous, so next time we see him, I might have to do a lot of groping and kissing you," he warned, a playful twinkle in his eyes.

"I don't mind that too much." Rosalie thought for a moment. "So this was the secret that you didn't want Kevin to tell?"

"Yes," he said shortly, obviously still angry at this blackmail situation. "Kevin is the only friend I have who knows about this. Apart from you."

"I'm your friend?"

"Yes. And my lover," he said, his voice dropping.

"Hah!"

"Jeez, not that 'hah' again."

"Don't worry about Robin, she's happy where she is and I hope I'm a good hostess."

"Yeah, she did mention about the late nights and loud music."

"Oh, Matt, you really have to spend the night at my house and see what it's like!" Rosalie said, laughing as she pictured Robin sitting in the corner, looking uncomfortable.

"I'd love to spend the night with you. The whole night," he said as he wagged his eyebrows at her

Nothing ventured, nothing gained

suggestively.
Rosalie laughed as she kissed him. "Well, I was thinking I could stay here."
"This is your home now."
"Huh?" she asked, her mouth open in shock.
"Joking. But it could be if you wanted it to be."
"Well...I haven't really thought...."
"Well," he said standing up, "think about it." He then grabbed her hand and pulled her along the corridor to what she assumed was his bedroom.
He closed the door and turned to look at her. "Do you have any idea how good you look standing there?"
"How about you tell me?" she suggested, reaching to unbutton his shirt. He watched her fingers for a while as they slid his shirt off his shoulders, then he looked up and saw her smiling.
"What?"
"Just....I love you."
His face softened in the darkness. "I love you too."
"Sorry for making you go crazy earlier."
He laughed as he pulled her shirt over her head. "Love is a crazy thing. So don't expect everything to be relaxed and sane now."
He gasped as she placed her hand on his hardness. "Nothing is ever going to be the same again," she whispered as she lifted her lips to his.
They kissed as they made their way to the double bed and landed with a heavy thump. Clothes soon became a distant thought as they stroked, touched, licked, sucked, explored each other's bodies, bringing each other to new heights of pleasure, which felt all the more right now they

were together.

"I love you. Christ I love you," Matthew groaned as he entered her and began to thrust. Rosalie looked up into his face and saw the concentration and pleasure in his eyes and she knew she'd never want another man as much as she wanted this one. She gave herself fully to him, surrendering to his moves. She loved him even more when he changed his rhythm and rotated his hips differently, and hit her clitoris causing her to scream with the sheer rapture of what he was doing and making her feel. She clenched around him when she came, taking him with her on a trip that was as exciting and heart trembling as it was calm and free. She felt him give himself up to the moment as well and at that point, it was as if they were one soul, experiencing the depths of what pure love really meant. Something too special to put into words.

Beth smiled as she walked away from where Matthew had told Rose about his past. After they had gone into his bedroom, she had descended the steps slowly and was now sitting in her chair. She knew Matthew would blame himself for her not telling him sooner about her health, but she also knew that tomorrow would be different. She would sit him down, tell him what she wanted to do. Which was, if God thought it right, to die peacefully. She didn't want to go, but she missed her husband to a point where it would be better for her to be in eternal peace. To see him again would mean everything to her, and although she

Nothing ventured, nothing gained

knew Matthew didn't really believe in God after what happened all those years ago, her faith had just been renewed by listening to Rose and Matthew. Love would exist beyond death, because Love was simply more powerful than Death could ever be. Beth had been querying that thought for a while, but seeing Rose and Matthew tonight, she knew there was no doubt that love overruled everything else. Which was why, if God took her, she wouldn't be afraid, because all she was doing was following her love through until the end.

Chapter thirteen

Thirteen months later

Everyone threw confetti over the bride and groom. They were a sight to behold as they descended the church steps one by one, smiling and joking with their guests, but casting each other private glances when they thought no one was looking. Rosalie laughed as Matthew picked her up in the traditional hold, making her laugh when he pretended to stagger forward, nearly dropping her. They made their way to the wedding car, awaiting their arrival outside Harpsden church, dressed in bows and ribbons. Matthew put Rosalie down and kissed her tenderly and lingering on the lips, earning yells and the flashes from cameras. They both separated, kissing cheeks and shaking hands with various people, thanking the priest who had performed the ceremony, but it wasn't too long before they found themselves at each other's sides again. Ever since Beth's death, Matthew had shown a vulnerable and child-like side to him, which Rosalie had come to love as much she loved his arrogance, which was rarely noticeable now. They had both supported each other this last year, and they found that they really couldn't ever be apart again. Especially not after experiencing and finding out how much they needed each other. After her first operation was a success, Beth had been well for five months, until the doctors had discovered that the cancer had spread to her lungs. She had died peacefully, at

Nothing ventured, nothing gained

home, with Matthew and Rosalie by her bedside, comforting her and reassuring her they would be fine. She had gone happily into the arms of her husband. Mathew had thrown himself into his work afterwards, telling Rosalie he was fine but pushing her away because he couldn't stand for her to see him weak. Until one night, when Rosalie had kindly and gently kissed him and asked him to tell her what he was feeling. She had comforted him all throughout the night as he cried. It was that night that they had discovered the depth of their love. But now, as Rosalie smiled and hugged Gwen and Neus together, she didn't think of that night, she thought of all the happy times they'd shared since then and how she was sure Beth would be glad that her son was finally happy.

She turned to Tili, standing with her arm around Neus, and hugged her too. Although she didn't know her very well, she was glad her brother had found someone who made him happy. Neus had told her about his and Tili's first attempt and had laughed until she cried. But apparently a few months later, they had met up again and fallen for each other. This time, Neus had assured her, he hadn't been inspected before their first time.

"I'm so proud, Lee," he said as she kissed him.

"Neus! Don't get soppy on me," she said as she playfully hit him. He just smiled and hugged her again.

"Look after yourself and visit. Every Sunday," he said. "Gwen has agreed to make us a roast dinner."

Rosalie laughed and nodded. "Wild horses

couldn't drag me away."

"Ah, the Rolling Stones" Neus said with a laugh, and then turned and kissed Tili gently on the mouth. He knew that when they had children, they wouldn't go into detail about their first date. He thought it strange how life tuned out. He winked at Robin, standing with baby Kurt Junior in her arms with Count Vicro at her side. Apparently he really did love Robin and was in so much pain when she left, that he had come to find her and married her regardless that she had given birth to a baby boy who belonged to someone else.

Kevin was the best man today and although he'd done the best man duties (which did consist of more than arranging the stag night, unlike what he had originally thought) he was now standing on Robin's other side, totally besotted with his son and on very good terms with Vicro and Robin. Robin was relieved it had turned out so well in the end and her father was coming round to the idea more quickly than she had ever expected. Mary turned towards the bride and smiled. She was glad Rosalie was happy, and was thankful for all the training they had done last summer after the disastrous dressage test at her horse show. Rosalie had been a firm teacher, but also complimentary and kind when Mary had felt low. She had been especially supportive during her divorce from Jack, after she had caught him cheating on her with a woman called Hooter. Now she was happy concentrating on Merlin and she allowed Rosalie to ride him whenever she wanted. It was Mary's way of paying Rosalie for the

Nothing ventured, nothing gained

lessons she gave her.

Rosalie turned to Gwen and felt her eyes welling up as Gwen dabbed her own.

"I'm sorry, Rose, I shouldn't cry, but you look so pretty."

"So do you."

"Gosh, I'm so sorry your parents couldn't be here," Gwen said as she touched Rosalie's arm. She nodded, ashamed at how her parents had behaved when she'd broken the news about her wedding.

"Don't worry too much if we can't get there" had been her father's words. She had slammed the phone down. She hadn't heard anything since and that had been six months ago.

"They are not my family. You and Neus are."

"And now Matthew," Gwen reminded her.

Rosalie rolled her eyes. "Yes and now Matthew. Could I forget my groom?"

"No, I don't suppose you could," Gwen said. Then after a minute she said, "Beth would be so pleased. This was her plan all along, you know, to find Matthew a wife before she left us."

Rosalie felt tears in her eyes and she smiled weakly, and then laughed. "Yes, the old girl always got what she wanted in the end."

"Rose, she told me how good you were for Matthew and she knew you were his soul mate. She also told me to tell you, on your wedding day…"

"But how did she know?"

Gwen smiled. "She had no doubt that you two would get married. She told me to tell you thank

you for confirming some of her thoughts and that she hoped Matthew looked after you and if not, put him in his place."
Rosalie laughed. "Oh God, I wish she were here."
"She is. She lives on in you two, but she wanted to be with her husband."
"What did I confirm?"
"She didn't tell me. She just smiled and then we talked about my bingo winnings."
Matthew came up to her side and put his arm around her. "I must take my bride away, the car is waiting," he said with a grin.
Rosalie quickly hugged Gwen and Matthew kissed her cheek.
They said one last goodbye and then got into the car and waited as it pulled away.
Rosalie turned to Matthew and smiled brightly.
"Happy?" he asked as he pulled back from kissing her.
"Well, you know, I suppose I am."
Matthew looked as if he was about to say something, but then he just took her hand and pulled it to his cheek.
"I love you," he said seriously.
"I love you too," she replied.
They settled back into their seats and held hands as they joked and kissed, not knowing what the future held for them, not knowing if the next step they took would be the right one or the wrong one. But they knew that together they could weather anything, because being together was when they were at their strongest.

Nothing ventured, nothing gained

www.ingramcontent.com/pod-product-compliance
Ingram Content Group UK Ltd.
Pitfield, Milton Keynes, MK11 3LW, UK
UKHW041227200426
11947UKWH00034B/41